STORIES
OF THE
BIBLE

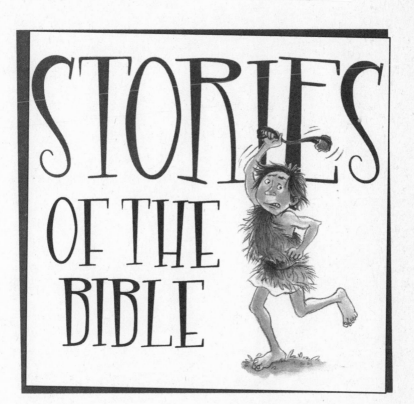

THE WORLD'S GREATEST

BIBLE PUZZLES

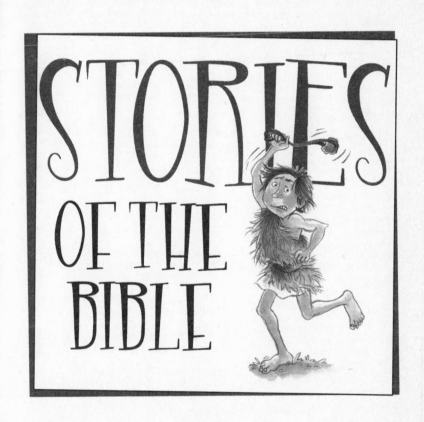

STORIES OF THE BIBLE

BARBOUR
PUBLISHING

ISBN 978-1-60260-029-4

Cover illustrator: Amy Wummer

Published by Barbour Publishing, Inc., P.O. Box 719, Uhrichsville, Ohio 44683
www.barbourbooks.com

Our mission is to publish and distribute inspirational products offering exceptional value and biblical encouragement to the masses.

Member of the
Evangelical Christian
Publishers Association

Welcome to the world's greatest collection of Bible puzzles

So you love the Bible? Enjoy word puzzles? Then this is the book for you!

Scattered throughout the pages of this book are eleven types of fun, challenging, and educational puzzles, all based on the world's greatest Book—the Bible. Exercise your knowledge of scripture and your puzzle-solving abilities as you work your way through the following puzzles:

Drop Twos (see page 7): Remove two letters from each seven-letter word in the left-hand column to create a new five-letter word (you may need to rearrange the remaining letters). Put the two dropped letters into the spaces to the right of the blanks. Then use these letters to spell out a phrase or sentence from the Bible.

Acrostics (see page 8): Read the definition in the left-hand column and write the word it describes in the right-hand column. Then place the coded letters from the right-hand column in the puzzle form following to spell out the verse indicated.

Word Searches (see page 10): Find and circle the search words in the puzzle grid—words may run forward, backward, up, down, and on the diagonal. When a scripture passage is given, find the words highlighted in **bold type**. If a phrase is underlined, those words are found together within the puzzle.

Cryptoscriptures (see page 12): Each of the cryptoscriptures is a Bible verse in substitution code. For example, JEHOVAH might become M P X S T Q X if M is substituted for J, P for E, X for H, and so on. One way to break the code is to look for repeated letters: E, T, A, O, N, R, and I are the most often used. A single letter is usually A or I. OF, IT, and IS are common two-letter words. Try THE and AND for a three-letter group. The code is different for each cryptoscripture. (There are two cryptoscriptures per page.)

Bible Sudoku (see page 13): Each 9 x 9 grid includes "givens," as with traditional sudoku puzzles. In this case, the givens are nine unique letters—which will spell out a biblical word or phrase. The nine-letter word or phrase is determined from the scripture printed below the puzzle. Solving the puzzle involves placing the nine letters in each row, column, and 3 x 3 minigrid (the white and shaded areas) so that no letter is duplicated in a row, column, or minigrid. Use your skills of deduction!

Crosswords (see page 14): Fill in the puzzle grid by starting answers in the appropriately-numbered boxes, and continuing either across to the right or down. Capitalized clues have answers that relate to the theme of the puzzle.

Scrambled Circles (see page 20): Unscramble the words from the list provided, placing the corrected words in the blanks corresponding with the numbers. Then use the circled letters to answer the question that follows.

Anagrams (see page 21): Unscramble the letters of the word or phrase given to create another word or phrase from the Bible.

Spotty Headlines (see page 26): Fill in the missing letters of each "headline," which relates to a Bible story. Then unscramble the letters you've added to the headline to form a name, which is the subject of the headline.

Telephone Scrambles (see page 27): Each set of telephone push-buttons contains a hidden Bible word—and you'll need to determine which letter of each combination is part of the word.

Bible Quotations (see page 32): Place the letters in each column into the puzzle grid preceding to form words. The letters may or may not fit into the grid in the same order in which they're given; black spaces indicate the ends of words. When a letter has been used, cross it off and do not use it again. When the grid has been properly filled in, you'll be able to read a Bible verse by scanning the lines of the grid from left to right.

Most clues are direct quotations are taken from the King James Version of the Bible, though some newer translations have also been referenced for variety. Puzzle answers begin on page 163.

Enjoy!

Born Again
JOHN 3:1

When others were sleeping, a man came to Jesus, curious as to what it meant for a grown man to be born again. Can you solve this puzzle to determine the name and position of this nighttime caller?

NETBALL	Sheep's cry	_____	1.	__ __
ISATINE	Smooth fabric	SATIN	2.	I E
CHARTED	Detested	HATED	3.	C R
PLATOON	Place flowers	_____	4.	__ __
FLANGED	Sharp corner	ANGLE	5.	F D
EGALITY	Cheerfully	_____	6.	__ __
MARCHED	Followed a curve	_____	7.	__ __
EPAULET	Shallow dish	_____	8.	__ __
JOBLESS	Tree trunks	_____	9.	__ __
EYEBALL	Stomach	_____	10.	__ __
WHARVES	Removed beard	_____	11.	__ __
STADIUM	Acknowledge	_____	12.	__ __

__ __ __ __ __ __ __ __ __ __ __ __

__ __ __ __ __ __ __ __ __ __ __ __
1 2 3 4 5 6 7 8 9 10 11 12

7

ACROSTIC
by Donna K. Maltese

Asp for Healing

Solve this acrostic to discover how Moses took the bite out of the people's gripping affliction.

What the snakes were described as (Numbers 21:6)

—— —— —— —— ——
40 34 18 4 25

Snakes bit the people because they'd done this
(Numbers 21:5–6)

—— —— —— —— —— —— —— —— —— ——
11 23 38 31 19 7 26 3 15 28

Full of poison

—— —— —— —— —— —— —— ——
10 29 17 35 2 39 21 8

Moses was a _____ of Christ

—— —— —— ——
30 12 24 6

To die

—— —— —— —— —— ——
16 5 20 32 37 9

Moses stood _____ God and the people

—— —— —— —— —— —— ——
27 36 1 14 22 13 33

7-17-28   38-23-8-15-8   38-7-28-36   7   37-6-20-31-6-

17-30   35-40   27-4-7-8-8,   7-3-28   16-21-1   26-1   21-

24-39-33   7   16-39-19-29,   7-3-28   26-1   11-7-38-29

1-35   16-7-8-8,   1-9-7-1   32-40   7   37-6-20-31-6-17-30

9-7-28   27-34-1-1-13-33   7-3-12   38-7-3,   14-9-22-33

9-5   27-18-9-18-19-28   1-9-5   37-6-20-31-6-17-30   35-

40   27-4-7-8-8,   9-5   19-34-10-5-28.

NUMBERS 21:9

9

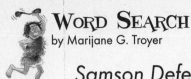

WORD SEARCH
by Marijane G. Troyer

Samson Defeats the Philistines
JUDGES 13–16

ASS
BARREN
CAMP
CARCASE
CHILD
DAGON
DAN
DELILAH
DRINK NOT
ENTICE
FIREBRANDS
FOXES
HEAD
HONEY
HOUSE FELL
JAWBONE
LAD
LEAN
LION

LORD
MANOAH
NAZARITE
OUT
PHILISTINES
PILLARS
RAZOR
RIDDLE
ROOF
SAMSON
TAIL
THREE HUNDRED
TOP
UNCLEAN
WIFE
WINE
WITH ALL HIS MIGHT
WOMAN

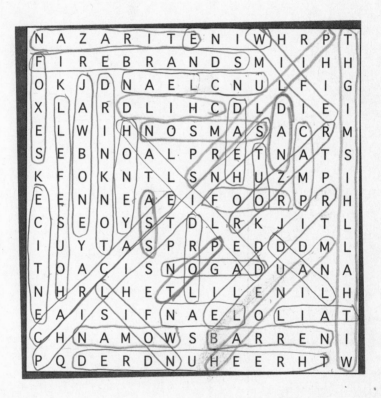

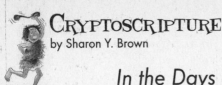

CRYPTOSCRIPTURE
by Sharon Y. Brown

In the Days of Noah

A vessel of the Lord's mercy, Noah followed God's instructions to a T. Solve these cryptoscriptures to learn more about God's pre-flood conversation with Noah, a man who was definitely on a learning curve—or, rather, a learning ark.

MEK XLK VMUK BEJL ELMO, JOR REK LA MHH

AHRVO UV FLZR SRALGR ZR; ALG JOR RMGJO

UV AUHHRK TUJO NULHREFR JOGLBXO JORZ;

MEK, SROLHK, U TUHH KRVJGLD JORZ TUJO JOR

RMGJO.

YXS VG WFWZP NEFEXA DCEXA VG YNN

GNWHC, DKV VG WFWZP HVZD HCYND DCVB

UZEXA EXDV DCW YZL, DV LWWT DCWO YNEFW

KEDC DCWW; DCWP HCYNN UW OYNW YXS

GWOYNW.

SECLFTDOA

Ehud's Death

EASY

	A	B	C	D	E	F	G	H	I
1	S	E	D	A	T	C	L	O	F
2	C	T	O	L	S	F	D	E	A
3	L	A	F	O	E	D	S	C	T
4	A	S	T	F	L	O	E	D	C
5	O	F	E	C	D	T	A	S	L
6	D	C	L	S	A	E	T	F	O
7	E	D	C	T	F	L	O	A	S
8	F	L	A	D	O	S	C	T	E
9	T	O	S	E	C	A	F	L	D

Hint: Column 9

"And the haft also went in after the blade; and the FAT CLOSED upon the blade, so that he could not draw the dagger out of his belly; and the dirt came out" (Judges 3:22).

13

CROSSWORD
by David K. Shortess

Climbing the Walls

Instead of climbing the walls—figuratively, of course—spend some time working this crossword. Then let the blessing of Psalm 122:7 sink into your heart and home: *"May there be peace within your walls and security within your citadels"* (NIV).

ACROSS

1   "_____ a mocker" (Proverbs 19:25 NIV)
5   "A swelling, _____ or a bright spot" (Leviticus 14:56 NIV) (2 words)
10 "Rehob, toward _____ Hamath" (Numbers 13:21 NIV)
14 "The scarlet cord in the window" (Joshua 2:21)
15 French river up north
16 "By _____ and living way" (Hebrews 10:20) (2 words)
17 LOCATION OF RAHAB'S HOUSE (Joshua 2:15) (4 words)
20 "Upon the great _____ of his right foot" (Leviticus 8:23)
21 "Have we not all _____ father?" (Malachi 2:10)
22 Formerly Shima Province, Japan, _____ prefecture
23 "And I _____ a vision" (Daniel 8:2) (2 words)
26 Follows *novel-* or *romantic-*
28 "_____ younger men as brothers" (1 Timothy 5:1 NIV)
30 WHAT EZEKIEL SAW BY THE DOOR OF THE COURT (Ezekiel 8:7) (5 words)
33 "Were cast into the _____ of fire" (Revelation 20:14)
34 "Behold, I will _____ new thing" (Isaiah 43:19) (2 words)
35 "To him that weareth the _____ clothing" (James 2:3)
36 Lincoln
37 Carnival workers
39 "I am like an _____ of the desert" (Psalm 102:6)
42 Sound from a massage recipient
43 Orthodontist's degree (abbr.)
44 "Am I _____, or a whale" (Job 7:12) (2 words)
45 WHERE THEY PUT THE BODY OF SAUL (1 Samuel 31:10) (3 words)
49 Salsa base
50 Another northern French river
51 "Thou hast asked _____ thing" (2 Kings 2:10) (2 words)
52 Follows *switcher-* and *tab-*
53 G. H. W. Bush was once its director
55 Greek *h*
56 WHERE EZEKIEL SAW CHERUBIMS AND PALM TREES (Ezekiel 41:20)
63 "The ants _____ people not strong" (Proverbs 30:25) (2 words)
64 "All of you be on the _____" (Joshua 8:4 NIV)
65 Relative of altitude (abbr.)
66 Hardy heroine
67 "From the tower of _____ shall they fall" (Ezekiel 30:6)
68 "And they shall _____" (Jeremiah 50:36)

DOWN

1   Winter bug
2   "They shoot out the _____" (Psalm 22:7)
3   "Beth Aven, lead _____ Benjamin" (Hosea 5:8 NIV) (2 words)
4   "And also of the _____" (Romans 2:9)
5   "_____ that setteth snares" (Jeremiah 5:26) (2 words)
6   "As light of foot as a wild _____" (2 Samuel 2:18)
7   Relative of quantity (abbr.)
8   "And I am a _____ man" (Genesis 27:11)
9   "Was _____ in stone" (Luke 23:53)
10 "Will not do the _____ of thy God" (Ezra 7:26)
11 Cloisonné covering
12 "The children of _____" (2 Chronicles 13:7)
13 Hooting chick

18 "Be with you now and change my
   ____" (Galatians 4:20 NIV)
19 "With so many the ____ not torn" (John
   21:11 NIV) (2 words)
23 "Which was the son of ____"
   (Luke 3:35)
24 Omri's son (1 Kings 16:28)
25 "Then I ____ up" (Genesis 41:21 NIV)
26 "Took thee ____ naked"
   (Matthew 25:38) (2 words)
27 "Which say, ____ thyself"
   (Isaiah 65:5) (2 words)
29 "Without a ____ of brightness?" (Amos
   5:20 NIV)
31 Utah neighbor
32 Discharge
37 Multicolored cat
38 July 15, for one
39 Government safety group (abbr.)
40 "Thou wilt surely ____ away" (Exodus
   18:18)
41 "Rowed hard to bring it to the
   ____" (Jonah 1:13)
42 "Hear, ____ ye people" (Micah 1:2)
44 Opposite of proud

45 "And said, ____ those with thee?"
   (Genesis 33:5) (2 words)
46 Bridal paths
47 Categorically
48 "For either he will ____ the one"
   (Matthew 6:24)
49 "Every ____ that which is before her"
   (Amos 4:3) (2 words)
54 "____ one people speaking the same
   language" (Genesis 11:6 NIV) (2 words)
55 Suffix meaning "little one"
57 ____ Cruces, NM
58 Haw's TV partner
59 Directional suffix
60 Arafat's group
61 "____ there be light" (Genesis 1:3)
62 Cain's mother (Genesis 4:1)

15

ACROSTIC
by Donna K. Maltese

Spinning Wheels

Crack the code to find out what wheels were spinning for Ezekiel when he witnessed this glorious sight!

A supernatural sight

<u> </u> <u> </u> <u> </u> <u> </u> <u> </u> <u> </u>
27   32   14   9   24   13

Where the Jews were in exile (Ezekiel 17:12)

<u> </u> <u> </u> <u> </u> <u> </u> <u> </u> <u> </u> <u> </u>
15   2   23   19   31   20   7

Ezekiel's calling (Ezekiel 2:5)

<u> </u> <u> </u> <u> </u> <u> </u> <u> </u> <u> </u> <u> </u>
26   3   12   21   8   16   1

Each being had four of these (Ezekiel 1:6)

<u> </u> <u> </u> <u> </u> <u> </u> <u> </u>
34   28   17   4   10

Each being also had four of these appendages (Ezekiel 1:6)

<u> </u> <u> </u> <u> </u> <u> </u> <u> </u>
6   30   25   11   18

Seeing this sight, Ezekiel must have been struck _____

<u> </u> <u> </u> <u> </u> <u> </u>
22   5   29   33

6-8-4-13   1-8-4   31-32-27-30-7-11   17-3-4-28-1-5-3-4-10

6-16-25-1,   1-8-4   6-8-4-4-31-18   6-16-25-1   23-19

1-8-4-29:   2-7-22   6-8-4-13   1-8-4   31-32-27-30-7-11

17-3-4-28-1-5-3-4-10   6-16-3-16   31-9-34-1-16-22   5-26

34-3-12-29   1-8-4   4-28-3-1-8,   1-8-4   6-8-4-4-31-14

6-16-3-16   31-9-34-1-16-22   5-21.

EZEKIEL 1:19

WORD SEARCH
by John Hudson Tiner

Ladder to Heaven
GENESIS 28:10–12

And **Jacob** went out **from Beersheba**, and **went toward Haran**. And he **lighted** upon a **certain** place, and **tarried there** all **night**, **because** the sun was set; and he **took** of the **stones** of that place, and put **them** for his **pillows**, and lay **down** in **that place** to **sleep**. And he **dreamed**, and behold a **ladder** set up on the **earth**, and the top of it **reached** to **heaven**: and **behold** the **angels** of God **ascending** and **descending** on it.

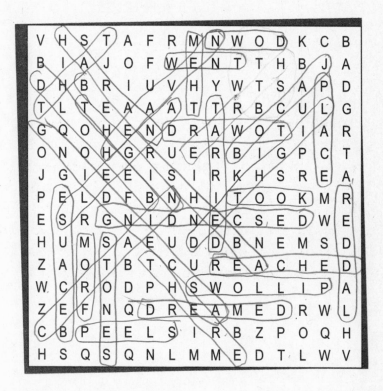

V	H	S	T	A	F	R	M	N	W	O	D	K	C	B
B	I	A	J	O	F	W	E	N	T	T	H	B	J	A
D	H	B	R	I	U	V	H	Y	W	T	S	A	P	D
T	L	T	E	A	A	A	T	T	R	B	C	U	L	G
G	Q	O	H	E	N	D	R	A	W	O	T	I	A	R
O	N	O	H	G	R	U	E	R	B	I	G	P	C	T
J	G	I	E	E	I	S	I	R	K	H	S	R	E	A
P	E	L	D	F	B	N	H	I	T	O	O	K	M	R
E	S	R	G	N	I	D	N	E	C	S	E	D	W	E
H	U	M	S	A	E	U	D	D	B	N	E	M	S	D
Z	A	O	T	B	T	C	U	R	E	A	C	H	E	D
W	C	R	O	D	P	H	S	W	O	L	L	I	P	A
Z	E	F	N	Q	D	R	E	A	M	E	D	R	W	L
C	B	P	E	E	L	S	I	R	B	Z	P	O	Q	H
H	S	Q	S	Q	N	L	M	M	E	D	T	L	W	V

SCRAMBLED CIRCLE
by Ken Save

Ah, Hindsight

When we begin to boast and brag, our comeuppance is only a stone's throw away.

1. AGTRE

2. EHOSSR

3. SLJUEOA

4. DTIMS

5. MJEELRAUS

6. TPELMUM

7. SHTOS

He should have ducked. Who was he?

1. ◯ _ _ _ _

2. _ ◯ _ _ _ _

3. _ _ _ ◯ _ _ _

4. _ ◯ _ _ _

5. _ _ _ _ _ ◯ _ _ _

6. _ _ _ _ _ _ ◯

7. ◯ _ _ _ _

Answer: _ _ _ _ _ _ _ _

Important Locales

Biblical events happened in biblical places—and these anagrammed locales hosted three of the Bible's greatest stories. Can you figure them out? Hint: The first two are Old Testament stories, the third a New Testament account.

Hen vine

_ _ _ _ _ _

A mantra tour

_ _ _ _ _   _ _ _ _ _ _

A sud scam

_ _ _ _ _ _ _ _

CROSSWORD
by Tonya Vilhauer

Beauty Contest

It's obvious that the adage "Beauty is only skin deep" did not apply to Esther. Solve this puzzle to discover more about this orphan girl who captured the hearts of her king and her people.

Esther obtained favour in the sight of all them that looked upon her.
ESTHER 2:15

ACROSS

1 ESTHER'S PEOPLE, WHOM HAMAN WANTED TO DESTROY (Esther 3:6)
5 "Thirty milch camels with their colts. . . and ten ____" (Genesis 32:15)
10 Popular cooking spray
13 Iraq's neighbor
14 2:1, for example
15 "I am the LORD, and there is none ____" (Isaiah 45:5)
16 Gambling game
17 A distinct smell
18 "AND THE ____ WAS FAIR AND BEAUTIFUL" (Esther 2:7)
19 Tempo (abbr.)
21 HE WAS ESTHER'S COUSIN (Esther 2:15)
23 "Four days ____ I was fasting until this hour" (Acts 10:30)
26 Dress edge
28 Athletic field
29 Trademark allergy medicine
32 Removes the water
33 Composer J. S.
34 Indian currency
36 Location
37 Cupid's dart
38 "And he shall pluck away his ____ with his feathers" (Leviticus 1:16)
42 Nothing (Latin)
43 Unsullied
44 ESTHER COULD NOT ENDURE SEEING ____ COME UPON THE JEWS (Esther 8:6)
46 "Who healeth all thy ____" (Psalm 103:3)
49 Malicious burning
51 PART OF ESTHER'S PURIFICATION RITUAL (Esther 2:12)
52 Time zone (abbr.)
53 "Was nothing ____, but rather grew worse" (Mark 5:26)
57 Football association (abbr.)
59 Throb
60 Love intensely
62 Voiced
66 Took to court
67 "____ a right spirit within me" (Psalm 51:10)
68 Electrical current unit
69 "Ye do ____, not knowing the scriptures" (Matthew 22:29)
70 THE WICKED HAMAN WAS ESTHER'S ADVERSARY AND ____ (Esther 7:6)
71 Dutch cheese

DOWN

1 Peanut butter brand
2 Epoch
3 "The children of Ammon made ____ against Israel" (Judges 11:4)
4 Stuck-up person
5 One who contrives evidence against an innocent person
6 "And all that handle the ____, the mariners" (Ezekiel 27:29)
7 Speck
8 Stretched car
9 Glide
10 "I will destroy your high ____" (Leviticus 26:30)

11 A native of the largest continent
12 "THE LADIES OF PERSIA AND _____"
    (Esther 1:18)
15 Nail filing board
20 Doctoral degree (abbr.)
22 "None is so fierce that _____ stir him
    up" (Job 41:10)
23 "Whereby we cry, _____, Father"
    (Romans 8:15)
24 Cogged wheel
25 "We are sanctified through. . Jesus
    Christ _____ for all" (Hebrews 10:10)
27 AN AROMATIC BALM GIVEN TO
    ESTHER (Esther 2:12) AND JESUS
    (Mark 15:23)
30 Eureka!
31 Shocking
32 "Who hath begotten the drops of
    _____?" (Job 38:28)
35 Childhood disease of FDR
37 Pain
38 Accountant (abbr.)
39 Tactic
40 Mined metals
41 Annoyance

42 "Were there not ten cleansed? but
    where are the _____?" (Luke 17:17)
44 THE KING LOVED HER "ABOVE ALL
    THE WOMEN" (Esther 2:17)
45 Picked a candidate
47 Stringy
48 Santa's helper
49 "Exalt him that is low, and _____ him
    that is high" (Ezekiel 21:26)
50 Happen again
54 "It is a _____ thing that the king
    requireth" (Daniel 2:11)
55 The first garden (Genesis 2:15)
56 THE KING ACCEPTED ESTHER'S
    REQUEST, AND IT WAS _____ (Esther
    9:14)
58 "Thou shalt _____ the LORD thy God"
    (Deuteronomy 11:1)
61 Phase of sleep (abbr.)
63 "He that spareth his _____ hateth his
    son" (Proverbs 13:24)
64 In the manner of (Fr.)
65 A mental system for permanently
    storing and recalling information later
    (abbr.)

ACROSTIC
by Donna K. Maltese

Miscommunication

When the sons of Adam set out to build a tower to heaven, God had other ideas. Crack the code to discover how "speaking in tongues" first evolved.

Not apart

$\overline{15}$ $\overline{7}$ $\overline{36}$ $\overline{30}$ $\overline{12}$ $\overline{26}$ $\overline{3}$ $\overline{20}$

Mankind

$\overline{4}$ $\overline{23}$ $\overline{31}$ $\overline{11}$ $\overline{16}$ $\overline{27}$

Construct

$\overline{22}$ $\overline{10}$ $\overline{17}$ $\overline{33}$ $\overline{2}$

Dialect

$\overline{28}$ $\overline{19}$ $\overline{6}$ $\overline{13}$ $\overline{24}$ $\overline{32}$

Disperse

$\overline{14}$ $\overline{29}$ $\overline{1}$ $\overline{9}$ $\overline{21}$ $\overline{34}$ $\overline{8}$

Thwart

$\overline{25}$ $\overline{35}$ $\overline{18}$ $\overline{5}$

15-4-3-8-3-25-7-8-3   17-14   9-4-3   6-1-31-30

7-25   18-12   29-11-5-5-32-2   22-1-22-34-33;

22-30-29-11-10-27-30   9-4-3   33-19-20-2

2-17-2   28-4-3-8-3   29-35-16-25-35-23-16-2

9-4-3   5-1-6-36-24-1-13-32   7-25   11-5-5   9-4-3

34-11-20-21-26.

GENESIS 11:9

SPOTTY HEADLINE
by Paul Kent and Sara Stoker

Battle Stories

The Bible is full of exciting military accounts. Can you determine who's behind each of the battle stories in these spotty headlines?

●ERIC●O FALLS TO GENERAL'●
●NORTHOD●X ATT●CK

— — — — — —

D●VID'S ●EAUTIFU● ●ON ●URDERED IN
C●UP ●TTEMPT

— — — — — — —

EGY●TIAN LE●DER'S MIG●TY A●MY
WAS●ED AW●Y, DR●WNED

— — — — — — —

TELEPHONE SCRAMBLE

by Nancy Bernhard

Conversions

We're not talking fractions here but of people who were brought into God's blessed family. Solve this telephone scramble to discover the names of these people who had a change of faith.

| PRS 7 | ABC 2 | TUV 8 | JKL 5 |

| PRS 7 | TUV 8 | TUV 8 | GHI 4 |

| PRS 7 | ABC 2 | MNO 6 | TUV 8 | DEF 3 | JKL 5 |

| ABC 2 | DEF 3 | MNO 6 | TUV 8 | TUV 8 | PRS 7 | GHI 4 | MNO 6 | MNO 6 |

| PRS 7 | TUV 8 | ABC 2 | JKL 5 | GHI 4 | ABC 2 | ABC 2 | MNO 6 |

| ABC 2 | ABC 2 | PRS 7 | ABC 2 | GHI 4 | ABC 2 | MNO 6 |

| ABC 2 | ABC 2 | MNO 6 | ABC 2 | ABC 2 | MNO 6 | GHI 4 | TUV 8 | DEF 3 |

WORD SEARCH
by Paul Kent

The Ark of the Covenant

BEZALEEL

CAPTURED

CHERUBIMS

DAVID

EKRON

ELI

EMERODS

FOUR RINGS

GLORY OF THE LORD

GOLD

HOPHNI

MERCY SEAT

MICE

OVERLAID

OXEN

PHILISTINES

PHINEHAS

SACRIFICING

SHEEP

SHITTIM WOOD

SOLOMON

STAVES

TEMPLE

TESTIMONY

WINGS

```
S G N I W P H I N E H A S Z A
L E L E E L A Z E B L T H W Q
A Y N O M I T S E T P I E C M
S M D P R J B R D C S P E N S
P X A Q H Y G A E B M I P T H
T H V S T F O U R R I N G S I
A O I O G V L F U C B O O D T
E P D L X M D P T A U R R O T
S H W O I E E R P H R K U R I
Y N A M X S N Q A M E E M I M
C I R O M N T V C I H L C W O
R T Y N Z W V I E C C P O E O
E E L P M E T O N E P D B R O
M S T A V E S O V E R L A I D
G N I C I F I R C A S W Q N K
```

CROSSWORD
by David K. Shortess

Nations in the Promised Land

With God on our side, no foes can stand in our way, no matter how fearsome or tenacious they be. Solve this puzzle to discover the enemies that God promised to oust if the Israelites remained obedient to Him alone.

I will. . .destroy all the people to whom thou shalt come.
EXODUS 23:27

ACROSS

1. "Now the ____ shall live by faith" (Hebrews 10:38)
5. Book after Micah
10. "And there ____ certain man at Lystra" (Acts 14:8) (2 words)
14. "No ____ will pitch his tent there" (Isaiah 13:20 NIV)
15. Enraged
16. A tenth of an ephah (Exodus 16:36)
17. A NATION ISRAEL ENCOUNTERED IN THE PROMISED LAND (Exodus 23:23)
19. "That nothing be ____" (John 6:12)
20. "____ woe is past" (Revelation 9:12)
21. ____ Moines, Iowa
22. "Which trieth our ____" (1 Thessalonians 2:4)
24. Wallet fillers
26. "Or if he shall ask an ____" (Luke 11:12)
29. Sprint rival
30. "He ____ to Moses" (Romans 9:15 NIV)
31. Growl
32. Bright tropical fish
35. Rocky hill
37. VIP transport
39. An age
40. "Come again?"
43. ANOTHER NATION FROM EXODUS 23:23
45. "And Jacob ____ pottage" (Genesis 25:29)
46. "It ____; be not afraid" (Matthew 14:27) (2 words)
47. "As if he blessed an ____" (Isaiah 66:3)
48. "He planteth an ____" (Isaiah 44:14)
50. "The apostles and the elders ____ consider this" (Acts 15:6 NIV) (2 words)
52. "I have ____ him to the LORD" (1 Samuel 1:28)
54. Dog's comments
58. KLM rival, once
59. Boston ____ Party
60. "By ____ rebuke I dry up the sea" (Isaiah 50:2 NIV) (2 words)
61. "Our houses to ____" (Lamentations 5:2)
64. Spread hay
66. "The wilderness of ____ (Exodus 16:1)
67. "Record this ____" (Ezekiel 24:2 NIV)
68. ANOTHER NATION FROM EXODUS 23:23
72. Got an A
73. "Behold, ____ was opened" (Revelation 4:1) (2 words)
74. Unit of heredity
75. "A ____ of meat from the king" (2 Samuel 11:8)
76. "The fortified ____ ruin" (Isaiah 25:2 NIV) (2 words)
77. Not evens

DOWN

1. "Now ____ well was there" (John 4:6)
2. Muse of astronomy
3. With rationality
4. Schedule abbreviation
5. "And ____ parts to dwell" (Nehemiah 11:1)
6. "That wicked men have ____ among you" (Deuteronomy 13:13 NIV)
7. Pass the ____ (take a collection)
8. Colorado native
9. "And he wanders into its ____" (Job 18:8 NIV)
10. "Let us ____ ourselves with loves" (Proverbs 7:18)
11. ANOTHER NATION FROM EXODUS 23:23
12. "But ____ the spirits to see" (1 John 4:1 NIV)

13 "Which used curious ____" (Acts 19:19)
18 Commercials
23 Decorate in relief
25 WWII craft (abbr.)
27 "Departed into ____" (Matthew 4:12)
28 Clamp together tightly, as teeth
31 Network
33 "Is there any thing ____ hard for me?" (Jeremiah 32:27)
34 "____ it came to pass" (Luke 2:1)
36 Akron resident
38 "And giveth ____ to her household" (Proverbs 31:15)
40 "For they all saw ____ " (Mark 6:50)
41 "But when ye pray, ____ not vain repetitions" (Matthew 6:7)
42 ANOTHER NATION FROM EXODUS 23:23
44 Unit of electrical potential
49 Canaan's father (Genesis 9:18)
51 Scotch fabrics
53 "O ____ not desired" (Zephaniah 2:1)
55 "And the land ____ from war" (Joshua 11:23)

56 "A ____ loveth at all times" (Proverbs 17:17)
57 "Have their ____ exercised to discern" (Hebrews 5:14)
60 Wood-cutting tool (var.)
61 Enos's grandfather (Luke 3:38)
62 "And thou shalt put it on a blue ____" (Exodus 28:37)
63 "He ____ on the ground" (John 9:6)
65 "And of ____ the priest, the scribe" (Nehemiah 12:26)
69 Former name of Tokyo
70 "And a ____ of new timber" (Ezra 6:4)
71 "Because ____ to the Father" (John 16:16) (2 words)

BIBLE QUOTATION
by Suzanne Stepp

Tested by Fire
DANIEL 3:25

When Shadrach, Meshach, and Abednego refused to worship a man-made idol, an enraged king's temperature rose. Solve this puzzle to discover what vision doused the flames of King Nebuchadnezzar's ire.

E	H	K	N	S	L	A	O	F	N	T	H
T	L	E	F	D	G	D	H	W	S	S	O
A	E	F	I	R	D	N	A	E	I	O	N
D	I	F	Y	I	S	H	S	F	F	R	H
E	O	E	O	D	E	S	N	O	E	T	W
O	H	A	R	U	H	T	N	O	U	T	
H	M	I	E	R	A	E	V	S	D	H	
L		H	O	G	M	E	I	A	E	E	
E		U	I	N	T	O	O	I	D	R	
		K	E	O	A	D			L		
		F	N	T							
		M		R							

DROP TWO
by Dorothy Pryse

Sowing Seeds
MATTHEW 13:4

Jesus often spoke in parables. Can you solve this drop two puzzle to uncover part of a parable Jesus planted in the minds of His listeners?

WIDOWER	More open	_____ 1. ___ ___
MATCHED	Performed	_____ 2. ___ ___
ENABLED	Dull	_____ 3. ___ ___
SNARING	Cereal	_____ 4. ___ ___
HOARDER	Devotion	_____ 5. ___ ___
EREMITE	Send money	_____ 6. ___ ___
SCANDAL	Manmade waterway	_____ 7. ___ ___
ONWARDS	Sketched	_____ 8. ___ ___
FROWNED	Male bee	_____ 9. ___ ___
ELEVATE	Male servant	_____ 10. ___ ___
DELIGHT	Octave	_____ 11. ___ ___
SCARLET	Container	_____ 12. ___ ___

— — — — — — — — — — — —
1 2 3 4 5 6 7 8 9 10 11 12

33

WORD SEARCH
by Connie Troyer

Stephen's Witness
ACTS 6–7

ASIA
BLASPHEMOUS
BLOOD
CAST OUT
CITY
COUNCIL
DISCIPLES
DISPUTING
EARS
FACE OF AN ANGEL
FALSE WITNESSES
FELL ASLEEP
FULL OF FAITH
GLORY
HEAVENS
HOLY GHOST

JERUSALEM
JESUS
LAMENTATION
LAW
LOUD
MARTYR
MIRACLES
MULTITUDE
RAIMENT
SAUL
SCATTERED
SLEW
STONED
WISDOM
WONDERS
WORD OF GOD

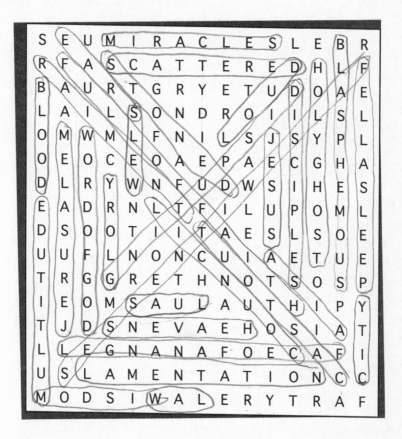

ACROSTIC
by Donna K. Maltese

Naaman's Lucky 7

A servant girl's advice led to a Syrian's healing. Crack the code to discover what Naaman had to do to become whole.

Naaman's military rank (2 Kings 5:1)

—— —— —— —— —— —— ——
38   33   23   7   18   12   5

Naaman's skin disease

—— —— —— —— —— —— ——
11   15   32   27   6   22   36

Prophet of Naaman's time (2 Kings 5:9)

—— —— —— —— —— ——
35   13   30   26   3   20

Another name for an Israelite

—— —— ——
24   2   16

Servant girl (2 Kings 5:2)

—— —— —— ——
17   8   29   1

What Naaman asked for, after his healing (2 Kings 5:18)

—— —— —— —— —— —— —— —— —— —— ——
9   34   31   25   4   19   14   28   10   21   37

7-3-10-28   16-35-28-7   3-10   1-34-16-28,   8-5-1   1-4-

23-32-15-1   3-12-17-22-14-11-9   21-2-19-2-5   7-29-17-

2-37   30-5   24-6-31-1-33-28,   20-38-38-6-27-1-4-5-25

7-34   7-3-10   26-18-36-4-5-25   34-9   7-3-10   17-8-5

34-9   25-6-1.

2 Kings 5:14

Jesus' Triumphal Entry

MEDIUM

	A	B	C	D	E	F	G	H	I
1									Y
2	K	S		Y		O		T	E
3	Y	N							D
4	E	A	Y		D		K		N
5	S		N	E				D	A
6		O	K						T
7	A	D				T	E		
8	N		O					A	K
9			E		Y		D		

Hint: Column E

Jesus _____ on a _____ while people threw down palm leaves before Him (John 12:13–14 NIV).

A Story for the Grandkids

Never forget God's works of wonder, but pass them on as everlasting remembrances.

1. NDSUMCEO

2. CKDMEO

3. MTNOU

4. LOEGRLAY

5. TRSTUO

6. EAFITMSN

7. EYAWR

8. FSLHE

A pile of stones would serve as a way to remember a special event.

1. _ _ _ _ _ O _ _

2. _ _ _ _ O _

3. O _ _ _ _ _

4. _ _ _ _ _ O _ _

5. _ _ _ _ O _

6. _ _ _ O _ _ _ _

7. _ _ O _ _

8. _ O _ _ _

Answer: _ _ _ _ _ _ _ _ _

CROSSWORD
by Sarah Lagerquist Simmons

Characters of Parables and Stories

God's Word is full of stories that teach us lessons and aid us in our walk with God. As you solve this puzzle, let the memories of Bible stories you've read and heard roam freely through your mind—in other words, no *tale*-gating!

"Son of man, give this riddle, and tell this story to the people of Israel."
EZEKIEL 17:2 NLT

ACROSS

1 "They practice divination like the Philistines and ____ hands with pagans" (Isaiah 2:6 NIV)
6 THIS TOMB-DWELLER "HAD DEVILS LONG TIME, AND ____ NO CLOTHES" (Luke 8:27)
10 "She dwelleth and abideth. . .upon the ____ of the rock" (Job 39:28)
14 "So the Egyptians made the children of Israel serve with ____" (Exodus 1:13 NKJV)
15 "You own the cosmos—you made everything in it, everything from ____ to archangel" (Psalm 89:11 MSG)
16 Mr. (Ger.)
17 An acid
18 A desert
19 "The ____ is not to the swift" (Ecclesiastes 9:11)
20 "THOU ART THE ____," NATHAN SAID TO DAVID AFTER REVEALING HIS SIN IN A PARABLE (2 Samuel 12:7)
21 "The LORD God caused a ____ sleep to fall upon Adam" (Genesis 2:21)
23 "They put Saul's armor on display. . . and placed his skull as a ____ in the temple of their god" (1 Chronicles 10:9 MSG)
25 THE PRODIGAL SON WAS EMPLOYED BY FEEDING THESE
26 Male turkey
27 An overbearing woman
30 HE EARNED HIS MASTER'S PRAISE BY MANAGING HIS MONEY WISELY (Luke 16)
34 Car model
35 THIS ____ WIDOW GAVE ALL SHE HAD (Mark 12:43)
36 Harridan

38 "These dreamers. . .revile and ____ and scoff at [heavenly] glories" (Jude 1:8 AMP)
39 Pull
40 Friend (Sp.)
42 Unsaturated carbon compound (suffix)
43 " 'Five gold tumors and five gold ____ ' " (1 Samuel 6:4 NIV)
44 Part of a mortise joint
45 Trollish
48 SAMSON WAS VERY ____
49 Female army corps (abbr.)
50 The Queen of Sheba told Solomon, "It was a ____ report that I heard. . .of thy acts and of thy wisdom" (1 Kings 10:6)
51 To stop the flow of blood
54 "It is a scabby sore of the head or ____" (Leviticus 13:30 NLT)
55 One millionth gram (abbr.)
58 English General in Revolutionary War
59 Republic in West Africa
61 U.S. State
63 Gelatin derived from algae
64 Related
65 JOSHUA'S TWO SPIES "CAME INTO A HARLOT'S HOUSE, ____ RAHAB" (Joshua 2:1)
66 SAMUEL'S "SONS WALKED NOT IN HIS ____, BUT TURNED ASIDE AFTER LUCRE" (1Samuel 8:3)
67 Back of neck
68 ONE OF JOB'S WOES: "NIGHT ____ AT MY BONES; THE PAIN NEVER LETS UP" (Job 30:16 MSG)

DOWN

1 Stuff
2 Bean
3 Opposed to (var.)

4 THE ELDEST ____ WAS JEALOUS (Luke 15)
5 RUNAWAY SON WHO LEFT HOME (Luke 15)
6 A DISPUTE ABOUT ____ WAS PART OF ONE PARABLE JESUS TOLD (Matthew 20)
7 Upon
8 THIEVES DID ____ A MAN IN THIS PARABLE (Luke 10)
9 Sender
10 Purity of a color
11 "I ____ where I sowed not" (Matthew 25:26)
12 Missouri's Gateway ____
13 Color of the Southern Confederates (var.)
22 Self-image
24 "The men did their best to ____ back to land" (Jonah 1:13 NIV)
25 "She shall shave her head, and ____ her nails" (Deuteronomy 21:12)
27 "The ____ of Siddim was full of slime pits" (Genesis 14:10)
28 Frosting
29 Male first name (var.)
30 "Abraham journeyed. . .toward the ____ country" (Genesis 20:1)
31 Garments

32 Herbivore (abbr.)
33 This idol fell before the Ark of the Covenant (1 Samuel 5:3)
35 Groups of parents and instructors (abbr.)
37 Bell
40 Adjusting
41 "You have made my days a ____ handbreadth" (Psalm 39:5 NIV)
43 HE BEGGED A DROP OF WATER FROM LAZARUS (Luke 16) (2 words)
46 ONE SLAVE GIRL EARNED MONEY FOR HER ____ BY FORTUNE-TELLING (Acts 16:16 NIV)
47 Computer (abbr.)
48 Title of respect in India
50 "Not my will, but ____" (Luke 22:42)
51 Band leader Artie
52 Roman apparel
53 "They sent him ____" (Genesis 12:20)
54 Fast pace
55 Mother's nickname
56 "Ye shall not eat of them that ____ the cud" (Deuteronomy 14:7)
57 "Ye shall be as ____" (Genesis 3:5)
60 Known also as (abbr.)
62 Jacob's son

41

WORD SEARCH
by Conover Swofford

God Is Faithful in the Old Testament

ACHOR	JIPHTHAHEL
AJALON	KEZIZ
BERACHAH	KINGS
CHARASHIM	MEGIDDO
CRAFTSMEN	MIZPEH
DECISION	MOUNTAINS
ELAH	PASSENGERS
ESCHOL	SALT
GERAR	SHITTIM
GIANTS	SLAUGHTER
GIBEON	SOREK
HAMONGOG	VISION
HEBRON	ZARED
HINNOM	ZEBOIM
JERICHO	ZEPHATHAH
JEZREEL	

O	H	P	Z	H	E	P	Z	I	M	I	O	B	E	Z
H	H	I	N	N	O	M	Z	O	D	D	I	G	E	M
Z	P	C	S	R	E	G	N	E	S	S	A	P	N	O
J	J	M	I	T	T	I	H	S	J	S	H	O	S	U
Z	H	E	B	R	O	N	P	H	A	A	L	G	J	N
H	H	S	O	R	E	K	J	L	T	A	N	R	Z	T
A	D	E	R	A	Z	J	T	H	J	I	J	L	L	A
M	M	M	R	O	H	C	A	A	K	J	K	Z	L	I
O	M	H	A	L	E	H	A	H	T	H	P	I	J	N
N	E	M	S	T	F	A	R	C	Z	I	Z	E	K	S
G	Z	R	E	T	H	G	U	A	L	S	L	L	T	J
O	P	E	M	I	H	S	A	R	A	H	C	N	Z	K
G	H	N	O	I	S	I	C	E	D	R	A	R	E	G
M	I	L	O	H	C	S	E	B	V	I	S	I	O	N
J	J	E	Z	R	E	E	L	J	G	I	B	E	O	N

TELEPHONE SCRAMBLE
by Connie Troyer

Thanks for Your Help

Wouldn't the world be great if everyone lived by the Golden Rule? Decipher the clues below to uncover the names of people who aided and abetted in a good way.

TUV	WXY	PRS	ABC	MNO	MNO	TUV	PRS
8	9	7	2	6	6	8	7

PRS	ABC	MNO	ABC	PRS	GHI	TUV	ABC	MNO
7	2	6	2	7	4	8	2	6

ABC	WXY	PRS	TUV	PRS
2	9	7	8	7

JKL	MNO	MNO	ABC	TUV	GHI	ABC	MNO
5	6	6	2	8	4	2	6

MNO	ABC	ABC	DEF	GHI	ABC	GHI
6	2	2	3	4	2	4

PRS	GHI	MNO	ABC	GHI
7	4	6	2	4

ABC	ABC	GHI	MNO	ABC	DEF	ABC	ABC
2	2	4	6	2	3	2	2

44

Before the Throne

Earthly rulers may die, but our King who reigns in heaven lives forever! Here's a prophet who saw God in all His glory. Can you crack the cryptoscripture codes to discover this humble man's heavenly vision?

WJ VAT GTML VAMV OWJF XCCWMA NWTN W

PMQ MSPB VAT SBLN PWVVWJF XEBJ M VALBJT,

AWFA MJN SWIVTN XE, MJN AWP VLMWJ

IWSSTN VAT VTYEST.

ABTC EGDR D, IHT DE QT! ZHW D GQ NCRHCT;

KTMGNET D GQ G QGC HZ NCMVTGC VDSE,

GCR D RITVV DC ABT QDREA HZ G STHSVT HZ

NCMVTGC VDSE: ZHW QDCT TJTE BGOT ETTC

ABT UDCY, ABT VHWR HZ BHEAE.

CROSSWORD
by David K. Shortess

Windows of Opportunity

Take this opportunity to see what these windows reveal to you.

Prove me now herewith, saith the LORD of hosts, if I will not open you the windows of heaven, and pour you out a blessing.

MALACHI 3:10

ACROSS

1 Victor's companion
4 Gun (the engine)
7 Volga feeder
10 "Much learning doth make thee ____" (Acts 26:24)
13 Swiss river (var.)
14 Of aircraft electrical systems
16 "But I am slow of speech, and ____ slow tongue" (Exodus 4:10) (2 words)
17 "And ____ them about thy neck" (Proverbs 6:21)
18 WHERE JEZEBEL WAS THROWN FROM A WINDOW AND DIED (2 Kings 9:30–33)
19 October follower (abbr.)
20 "Whether he be a sinner ____, I know not" (John 9:25) (2 words)
22 "God: ____ me according to thy mercy" (Psalm 109:26) (2 words)
23 Meaning three (comb. form)
24 WHERE A RAVEN AND A DOVE WERE RELEASED FROM A WINDOW (Genesis 8:6–8) (2 words)
27 Responded vocally to a tongue depressor
29 Baseball great Ott
30 Rockies and Cascades (abbr.)
32 "And ____ did that which was right in the eyes of the LORD" (1 Kings 15:11)
35 Click beetle
38 "Take thee a ____, and lay it before thee" (Ezekiel 4:1)
42 THE DIRECTION DANIEL'S WINDOWS FACED (Daniel 6:10) (2 words)
45 Part of CEO (abbr.)
46 "She gave me some fruit from the tree, and ____" (Genesis 3:12 NIV) (3 words)
47 "Your lightning ____ up the world" (Psalm 77:18 NIV)
48 ____-do-well (slang)
50 "Unto us a ____ is given" (Isaiah 9:6)

52 "And took a ____, and girded himself" (John 13:4)
55 WHERE PAUL ESCAPED THROUGH A WINDOW (2 Corinthians 11:32–33)
60 "For ye tithe mint and ____ and all" (Luke 11:42)
61 Muslim women's garments
64 "His children, their ____ is the sword" (Job 27:14 NIV)
65 Similar to O.C.S. (abbr.)
66 WHERE RAHAB TIED A THREAD IN A WINDOW (Joshua 2:1–21)
69 "He maketh me to ____ down in green pastures" (Psalm 23:2)
70 "As though I shot ____ mark" (1 Samuel 20:20) (2 words)
71 "Therefore I said, Surely these ____ " (Jeremiah 5:4) (2 words)
72 Shimei's father (1 Kings 4:18 NIV)
73 "They that ____ in tears shall reap in joy" (Psalm 126:5)
74 "And ____ him in the sand" (Exodus 2:12)
75 Oolong or mint
76 "In the Valley of ____ Hinnom" (2 Kings 23:10 NIV)

DOWN

1 Betray (2 words, slang)
2 Capital on the Nile
3 "Men condemned to die in the ____" (1 Corinthians 4:9 NIV)
4 British rule in India
5 Grandmother of Enos (Genesis 4:25–26)
6 Eyeshade (var.)
7 "To every ____ loaf of bread" (1 Chronicles 16:3) (2 words)
8 Capital of Ukraine
9 "Create in me ____ heart, O God" (Psalm 51:10) (2 words)
10 "Which is the ____ Adar" (Esther 8:12)

11 "As I wrote _____ in few words" (Ephesians 3:3)

12 WHO MICHAL LET DOWN FROM A WINDOW (1 Samuel 19:12)

15 Russian city on the Ural River

21 Bit of electrical resistance

25 Soothsayer or clairvoyant

26 "For as in Adam _____ " (1 Corinthians 15:22) (2 words)

28 Nick and Nora Charles's cinematic pup

30 "Are you not _____ men" (1 Corinthians 3:4 NIV)

31 Self-evident verity

32 "And _____ the sacrifices of the dead" (Psalm 106:28)

33 Red or white in baseball

34 "Stand in _____, and sin not" (Psalm 4:4)

36 "Go into the city, and a man carrying _____ of water will meet you" (Mark 14:13 NIV) (2 words)

37 Vietnamese holiday

39 "Wherefore dealt ye so _____ with me" (Genesis 43:6)

40 Island garland

41 9-1-1 responder (abbr.)

43 Teen bane

44 Greek portico

49 He slew 450 prophets of Baal (1 Kings 18:40)

51 It may cause a check to bounce (abbr.)

52 WHERE EUTYCHUS WENT TO SLEEP AND FELL FROM A WINDOW (Acts 20:6–9)

53 "And led him _____ crucify him" (Mark 15:20) (2 words)

54 "And there _____ the giants, the sons of Anak" (Numbers 13:33) (2 words)

55 "The mountains will _____ new wine" (Joel 3:18 NIV)

56 It's a tie

57 One of the twelve spies (Numbers 13:6)

58 Useful

59 "And thou shalt _____ enemy in my habitation" (1 Samuel 2:32) (2 words)

62 A son of Jeduthun (1 Chronicles 25:3)

63 "That they bring thee _____ heifer" (Numbers 19:2) (2 words)

67 "Once cultivated by the _____ " (Isaiah 7:25 NIV)

68 "Or athirst, _____ stranger" (Matthew 25:44) (2 words)

ACROSTIC
by Donna K. Maltese

A Gated Community

Decipher this puzzle to discover John's description of the gated community of New Jerusalem. Sounds priceless!

John was one of twelve

<u> </u> <u> </u> <u> </u> <u> </u> <u> </u> <u> </u> <u> </u> <u> </u>
2   14   28   19   37   10   3   6

A revelation

<u> </u> <u> </u> <u> </u> <u> </u> <u> </u> <u> </u>
20   39   31   5   11   18

Precious stones _____ the new city's walls (Revelation 21:19)

<u> </u> <u> </u> <u> </u> <u> </u> <u> </u> <u> </u> <u> </u> <u> </u> <u> </u>
43   36   7   16   23   1   32   8   29

A translucent variety of quartz (Revelation 21:19)

<u> </u> <u> </u> <u> </u> <u> </u> <u> </u> <u> </u> <u> </u> <u> </u> <u> </u> <u> </u>
17   25   42   38   24   12   46   40   35   21

The words John wrote were true and _____ (Revelation 21:5)

<u> </u> <u> </u> <u> </u> <u> </u> <u> </u> <u> </u> <u> </u> <u> </u>
26   13   47   44   33   4   22   30

Number of tribes of Israel

<u> </u> <u> </u> <u> </u> <u> </u> <u> </u> <u> </u>
9   45   15   41   34   27

9-33-8   44-45-3-10-20-3   43-13-37-12-6   45-8-7-8

44-45-3-10-20-3   14-27-42-7-38-31:   3-34-3-7-21

31-3-34-3-7-36-41   43-13-37-12   45-2-1   11-4   40-18-15

14-27-42-7-38:   2-16-29   9-33-8   31-9-7-3-3-9   11-26

9-32-8   17-5-9-21   45-2-1   14-22-7-12   43-28-30-46,

2-1   39-9   45-8-7-8   9-7-36-35-19-14-36-7-15-35-9

43-10-36-6-6.

REVELATION 21:21

BIBLE QUOTATION
by Suzanne Stepp

An Even Exchange
GENESIS 22:13

God is always there for us, but we must be watchful to see where He's working. Solve this puzzle to discover how God provided for a faithful man just in the nick of time.

N	I	D	F	H	F	R	D	T	S	E	A
E	N	C	E	A	O	F	M	A	I	R	G
M	O	I	F	B	H	D	S	T	B	N	A
A	U	B	A	I	R	A	E	A	H	O	A
D	N	T	E	U	H	I	D	R	O	N	D
I	T	P	H	O	R	E	T	A	I	B	K
R	N	F	S	T	H	H	R	S	M	N	W
	D	H	A	F	R	A	E	N	S	I	Y
		O		E	C	E	H		T	B	H
		T			I	M				E	N
		N			O	L				O	U
					G	K					M

SPOTTY HEADLINE
by Paul Kent and Sara Stoker

Government Intrigue

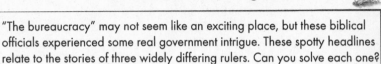

"The bureaucracy" may not seem like an exciting place, but these biblical officials experienced some real government intrigue. These spotty headlines relate to the stories of three widely differing rulers. Can you solve each one?

⬤ULER SLAUG⬤TERE⬤ ALL MALE BABIES IN H⬤PE OF ⬤LIMINATING FUTURE KING

— — — — —

MAN HO⬤ELESSLY ⬤RI⬤S TO ER⬤SE B⬤AME W⬤TH HAND WASHING

— — — — — —

GOV⬤RNMENT OFF⬤CI⬤L SPEN⬤S ⬤IGHT WITH ⬤IONS

— — — — — —

WORD SEARCH
by Conover Swofford

God Is Faithful in the New Testament

ANANIAS
BARNABAS
CORNELIUS
DORCAS
ELISABETH
EUNICE
JOSEPH [OF
    ARIMATHAEA]
LAZARUS
LOIS
LYDIA
MARTHA
MARY
NICANOR
NICODEMUS

NICOLAS
ONESIMUS
PARMENAS
PAUL
PHEBE
PHILIP
PROCHORUS
SILAS
STEPHEN
TABITHA
TIMON
TIMOTHEUS
TITUS
WITNESS
ZACCHAEUS

```
T I M O T H E U S A I D Y L O
I A P I L I H P R O N A C I N
M H B P A R M E N A S O M I E
O T S I M N E H P E T S C M S
N R A O T A C H O S A O O A I
I A B E J H T H I L D A M R M
C M A C M O A L S E M A K Y U
O I N I S E A U M D O R C A S
L P R N T S E U K L U A P J U
A S A U H A S S E N T I W O R
S E B E H P R O C H O R U S A
S H M C O H T E B A S I L E Z
H M C X O S L O I S W S S P A
S A N A N I A S U T I T W H L
Z T O L T S S U I L E N R O C
```

CROSSWORD
by Sarah Lagerquist Simmons

Animal Stories

God made animals that serve, sustain, and challenge us. Solve this puzzle to uncover some amazing and memorable stories of the creatures with which God has blessed us and this earth.

God made the wild animals according to their kinds, the livestock according to their kinds, and all the creatures that move along the ground according to their kinds. And God saw that it was good.

GENESIS 1:25 NIV

ACROSS

1 Pulpy residue left after pressing grapes
5 Group of three feathers in a bird's wing
10 Sandwich (abbr.)
13 Toad species
14 Highland musician
15 Knife
16 Carol: "The First ____"
17 Form of oxygen
18 "COME THOU. . .____ THE ARK" (Genesis 7:1)
19 Money group (abbr.)
21 MOST FAMOUS BIBLE ANIMAL STORY (2 words)
23 Tunisian Cape
26 Legume seed
28 Jots
29 Terse maxim
32 Mountain in Sicily
33 Suitor
34 "A SHEPHERD DIVIDETH HIS SHEEP FROM THE ____" (Matthew 25:32)
36 Pain
37 Persona non ____
38 Move
42 "DANIEL IN THE ____ DEN" IS ANOTHER WELL-KNOWN BIBLE ANIMAL STORY
43 Michigan's neighbor
44 THE ____ FELL FOR 40 DAYS DURING THE FLOOD
46 Withdrawing
49 Mission in Texas
51 Summer month (abbr.)
52 Organization linking parents and schools
53 "Soldiers likewise ____ of him" (Luke 3:14)
57 Unit of weight
59 Propellers
60 Smells
62 Humorist Bombeck
66 Siblings (abbr.)
67 Bestow
68 "The ____ out of the wood doth waste it" (Psalm 80:13)
69 AT THE ____ OF A STORY ABOUT A MAN AND HIS SHEEP, DAVID REPENTED
70 "Twelve lions stood. . .upon the six ____" (1 Kings 10:20)
71 German Roman Catholic theologian Johann

DOWN

1 IF IT HAD NOT BEEN FOR HIS DONKEY, BALAAM WOULD HAVE BEEN A DEAD ____
2 "Four days ____ I was fasting" (Acts 10:30)
3 Repent
4 THIS ANIMAL WAS KILLED FOR A FEAST (Luke 15:23)
5 Pinnacle
6 Girl's name, for short
7 JESUS CAME RIDING INTO JERUSALEM, SITTING ____ A DONKEY
8 Weave structure
9 Region

10	Music for one or two solo instruments
11	Excessive
12	"Many. . .brought their _____ together, and burned them" (Acts 19:19)
15	Once roamed the northern plains of the U.S.
20	Speedometer reading (abbr.)
22	Visits to a Web site
23	Leavened cake
24	Oil cartel (abbr.)
25	HE SPENT UP TO 100 YEARS BUILDING A BOAT FOR HIS FAMILY AND ANIMALS
27	Violent behavior
30	Day of the week (abbr., var.)
31	Groans
32	Seventh letter of Greek alphabet (abbr.)
35	On the ocean (2 words)
37	Snare
38	Home-building material for pioneers
39	"A _____ for the horse, a bridle for the ass" (Proverbs 26:3)
40	Uneducated speech includes this word for "am not"
41	Exercise
42	WHAT SAMSON KILLED WITH HIS BARE HANDS
44	Used for cleaning a muzzle
45	Accumulate
47	"He _____ off every branch. . .that bears no fruit" (John 15:2 NIV)
48	Conceit
49	Sun-dried brick of clay
50	STORIES IN THE BIBLE ARE TOLD SO THAT WE CAN _____ A LESSON
54	ELIJAH PROPHESIED THAT _____ WOULD EAT WICKED QUEEN JEZEBEL (2 Kings 9:36)
55	Revise
56	BIRD SENT FROM THE ARK
58	Cornhusker State (abbr.)
61	Salesman (abbr.)
63	"Ashahel was as light of foot as a wild _____" (2 Samuel 2:18)
64	Raincoat (abbr.)
65	WHAT SAVED NOAH'S FAMILY AND THE ANIMALS

ACROSTIC
by Connie Troyer

A Story, a Story

God's Word was written to be read. Solve this puzzle to uncover its purpose and how it can change our mindset.

Displaced queen (Esther 1:19)

$\overline{8}$ $\overline{18}$ $\overline{33}$ $\overline{26}$ $\overline{1}$ $\overline{36}$

Six safe places in Palestine (Numbers 35:9–11; Joshua 20:7–9)

$\overline{9}$ $\overline{59}$ $\overline{20}$ $\overline{52}$ $\overline{47}$ $\overline{13}$ $\overline{28}$ $\overline{57}$

$\overline{15}$ $\overline{53}$ $\overline{29}$ $\overline{35}$ $\overline{23}$ $\overline{51}$

Samson was set apart as this (Judges 13:5, 24)

$\overline{12}$ $\overline{38}$ $\overline{14}$ $\overline{48}$ $\overline{3}$ $\overline{55}$ $\overline{32}$ $\overline{25}$

Jonathan's crippled son (2 Samuel 4:4)

$\overline{6}$ $\overline{41}$ $\overline{16}$ $\overline{46}$ $\overline{58}$ $\overline{24}$ $\overline{2}$ $\overline{54}$ $\overline{56}$ $\overline{17}$ $\overline{22}$ $\overline{40}$

The last plague (Exodus 11:1, 5)

$\overline{10}$ $\overline{27}$ $\overline{49}$ $\overline{39}$ $\overline{50}$ $\overline{30}$ $\overline{2}$ $\overline{44}$ $\overline{21}$

A well appeared here for Hagar (Genesis 21:14–21)

$\overline{31}$ $\overline{7}$ $\overline{5}$ $\overline{11}$ $\overline{43}$ $\overline{34}$ $\overline{37}$ $\overline{4}$ $\overline{19}$ $\overline{45}$

10-2-15   31-26-48-1-39-28-17-8-47-44

32-46-7-21-23-19   31-25-44-4   31-49-55-32-50-25-37

18-10-2-44-53-32-36-6-51   31-51-15-41

31-34-27-50-20-47-21   10-28-49   28-35-15

5-51-48-44-12-59-21-23,   50-40-18-22   31-17

32-46-3-2-35-23-40   16-38-32-58-53-12-9-43

48-37-11   9-42-6-29-42-3-20   28-57   20-40-4

13-9-3-55-16-22-35-34-4-54   6-52-23-46-22   26-38-8-17

26-2-16-25.

ROMANS 15:4

ANAGRAM
by Paul Kent

More Important Locales

As we've already noted, Biblical events happened in biblical places—and these anagrammed spots hosted three more of the Bible's greatest stories. Can you figure them out? Hint: The first two are Old Testament stories, the third a New Testament account.

Need of danger

_ _ _ _ _ _   _ _   _ _ _ _

Rich Joe

_ _ _ _ _ _ _

O lost movie fun

_ _ _ _ _   _ _   _ _ _ _ _ _

Water Provided
SEE EXODUS 17:6

You can't get water from a stone. . .or can you? Solve this puzzle to find out what God told Moses to do in order to quench the thirst of His people.

SCALENE	Not dirty	_____ 1. ___ ___
MIDMOST	Surrounded by	_____ 2. ___ ___
PIANIST	Discolor	_____ 3. ___ ___
TACKLER	Squeak	_____ 4. ___ ___
EYEHOLE	Full of holes	_____ 5. ___ ___
MOBSTER	Judge's garments	_____ 6. ___ ___
HEADMAN	Described	_____ 7. ___ ___
ENDWAYS	Batons	_____ 8. ___ ___
RAMBLED	Accuse	_____ 9. ___ ___
RAZORED	Demolished	_____ 10. ___ ___
TITANIC	Corrupt	_____ 11. ___ ___
KNITTER	Hackneyed	_____ 12. ___ ___
PRICKET	An instant	_____ 13. ___ ___

___ ___ ___ ___ ___ ___ ___ ___ ___ ___ ___ ___ ___

1 2 3 4 5 6 7 8 9 10 11 12 13

WORD SEARCH
by David Austin

Joseph and Mary
LUKE 1–2

ANGEL
APPEAR
APPEARED
AUGUSTUS
BETHLEHEM
BIRTH
CAESAR
DREAM
ELIZABETH
EMMANUEL
GABRIEL

GLORY
JESUS
JOSEPH
MARY
MESSIAH
NAZARETH
PEACE
PROPHECY
PROPHET
SHEPHERDS
ZECHARIAH

WORD SEARCH
by David Austin
(continued)

```
A  J  T  M  V  N  H  E  E  S  S  G  C
U  D  T  S  E  B  A  L  T  M  H  L  E
G  A  E  B  I  S  I  Z  R  M  E  O  D
U  K  P  R  E  Z  S  A  A  A  P  R  P
S  L  T  P  A  T  S  I  W  R  H  Y  R
T  H  K  B  E  E  H  E  A  Y  E  E  O
U  G  E  E  A  A  P  L  H  H  R  T  P
S  T  O  C  C  J  R  P  E  U  D  Q  H
H  Z  E  C  H  A  R  I  A  H  S  J  E
E  M  M  A  N  U  E  L  F  N  E  B  C
Z  H  P  E  S  O  J  P  F  Q  G  M  Y
L  E  I  R  B  A  G  A  S  U  S  E  J
T  E  H  P  O  R  P  D  R  E  A  M  L
```

CROSSWORD
by David K. Shortess

Three Monetary Lessons

The three theme answers are possible titles for the three lessons cited, all dealing with coins.

Sell all that thou hast, and distribute unto the poor,
and thou shalt have treasure in heaven.
LUKE 18:22

ACROSS

1 "An ____ pleasing to the LORD" (Leviticus 1:9 NIV)
6 Transcript data (abbr.)
9 "Crying, ____, Father" (Galatians 4:6)
13 Largest Philippine island
14 "Eat not of it ____, nor sodden" (Exodus 12:9)
15 Chunk of earth
16 LESSON 1: WHEN A SINNER REPENTS (Luke 15:8–10 NIV) (4 words)
19 Daily Planet reporter
20 "He ____ and worshipped him" (Mark 5:6)
21 "Men condemned to die in the ____" (1 Corinthians 4:9 NIV)
22 "How long will it be ____ they believe me" (Numbers 14:11)
23 Valley of ____ Hinnom (Joshua 18:16 NIV)
24 "Walking after their ____ lusts" (Jude 1:16)
25 Links gadget
26 Sure competitor?
27 ____ Mahal
30 Get soaked?
33 Obtain
34 Woody's son
35 LESSON 2: ON THE PAYING OF TAXES (Matthew 17:27 NIV) (5 words)
38 "From the lions' ____" (Song of Solomon 4:8)
39 "You may know the hope to which he ____ called you" (Ephesians 1:18 NIV)
40 Philistines' god (Judges 16:23)
41 112° 30' from N
42 "Their conscience seared with a ____ iron" (1 Timothy 4:2)

43 "____ it is written" (Matthew 4:6)
44 "And the ____ of Carmel shall wither" (Amos 1:2)
45 Push hard
46 Mineral spring
49 "And ____ Aaron of his garments" (Numbers 20:26)
52 "A wise ____ maketh a glad father" (Proverbs 10:1)
53 ____ Street
54 LESSON 3: TRUE SACRIFICE (Mark 12:41–44) (3 words)
57 "They ____ perverse and crooked generation" (Deuteronomy 32:5) (2 words)
58 "____ no man any thing" (Romans 13:8)
59 Esso competitor
60 Signs of spring
61 "For our ____ is come" (Lamentations 4:18)
62 "She maketh fine ____" (Proverbs 31:24)

DOWN

1 "Cast alive into ____ of fire" (Revelation 19:20) (2 words)
2 "I will make thee ____ over many things" (Matthew 25:21)
3 Earth's natural UV blocking layer
4 "It is ____ holy unto the LORD" (Exodus 30:10)
5 "Go to the ____" (Proverbs 6:6)
6 "For in this we ____" (2 Corinthians 5:2)
7 "The ____ as of a woman in travail" (Jeremiah 22:23)
8 Rye bristle
9 Sign of fall

1	2	3	4	5		6	7	8		9	10	11	12
13						14				15			
16				17				18					
19				20			21						
22			23			24							
		25			26				27	28	29		
30	31	32		33			34						
35				36		37							
38			39			40							
41			42		43								
	44			45			46	47	48				
49	50	51		52		53							
54			55			56							
57			58			59							
60			61			62							

10 "And he made a vail of ____" (Exodus 36:35)

11 Former capital of West Germany

12 "Then he shall ____ fifth part" (Leviticus 27:13) (2 words)

17 Manitoba tribe

18 Forest youngster

23 ____ there, done that

24 "And again he denied with an ____" (Matthew 26:72)

25 "Give us ____ day our daily bread" (Matthew 6:11)

26 All ____ are off

27 Math branch

28 "Sweeter ____ than honey" (Psalm 19:10)

29 Zebedee's son (Matthew 10:2)

30 Said (arch.)

31 Hits a hole-in-one

32 Musical sound

33 Pest

34 "So is good news from ____ country" (Proverbs 25:25) (2 words)

36 Where "pancake" is understood (abbr.)

37 Esau's land

42 Arizona tribe

43 "Who ____ the coals into flame" (Isaiah 54:16 NIV)

44 Natives of northern New Mexico

45 "Nevertheless the men ____ hard" (Jonah 1:13)

46 "And ____ the right hand of God" (Mark 16:19) (2 words)

47 ____ work (such as sewing)

48 "Happy Days" actor Williams

49 Pierce

50 "No ____ Street"

51 "A ____ shaken with the wind" (Matthew 11:7)

52 "That which was ____ in his heart" (Matthew 13:19)

53 "La Boheme" role

55 "A loving ____, a graceful deer" (Proverbs 5:19 NIV)

56 Last O.T. book

SCRAMBLED CIRCLE
by Suzanne Stepp

Would You Want This Job?

By the simplest, humblest acts of service, we can show our greatest love.

1. LOTEW
2. SGATMRNE
3. NDAH
4. HDEA

5. ESDIA
6. ARTWE
7. RUOH
8. IWEP

9. DDRIEG
10. SFATE
11. UPRSPE
12. ATRP

Jesus acted as His disciples' servant.

1. _ _ O _ _
2. _ O _ _ _ _ _ O
3. O _ _ _
4. _ O _ _
5. _ _ _ O _
6. _ _ O _ _
7. O _ _ _
8. _ _ _ O
9. _ O O _ _ _
10. O O _ _ _
11. _ _ _ _ O _
12. _ _ _ O

Answer: _ _ _ _ _ _ _ _ _ _ _ _ _ _ _ _

by Connie Troyer

Sound the Trumpets

The word *trumpet* is mentioned sixty-six times in the Bible. Solve this puzzle to find out how this blaringly evident instrument has been used.

PRS 7	PRS 7	ABC 2	GHI 4	PRS 7	DEF 3	

JKL 5	DEF 3	PRS 7	GHI 4	ABC 2	GHI 4	MNO 6

WXY 9	ABC 2	PRS 7	MNO 6	GHI 4	MNO 6	GHI 4

WXY 9	GHI 4	MNO 6	MNO 6

ABC 2	MNO 6	GHI 4	DEF 3	JKL 5	PRS 7

JKL 5	TUV 8	ABC 2	GHI 4	JKL 5	DEF 3	DEF 3

DEF 3	PRS 7	GHI 4	PRS 7	ABC 2	GHI 4	MNO 6

GHI 4	ABC 2	TUV 8	GHI 4	DEF 3	PRS 7

A Sign of Things to Come

With God's help via the prophet Isaiah, an ailing Hezekiah was given a sign of his immanent healing. Crack the code with 2 Chronicles 32 to learn more about this good king who, after regaining his health, spent his remaining years in prosperity.

Hezekiah was ____ of Judah

—— —— —— ——
26   9   1   17

Isaiah's father

—— —— —— ——
6   12   18   24

Hezekiah and his city were delivered from the king of this country

—— —— —— —— —— —— ——
15   23   8   38   33   29   2

To have regained health

—— —— —— —— —— —— —— —— ——
27   14   36   30   19   10   22   34   7

Aid

—— —— —— ——
4   13   21   32

Hezekiah rerouted the ____ of Gihon

—— —— —— —— —— —— —— —— —— —— ——
16 28 5 35 25 37 11 20 39 31 3

29-1   5-4-18-31-14   7-15-38-23   4-3-24-3-26-9-28-4

16-2-23   8-9-37-26   5-30   5-4-10   7-13-28-5-4,   6-1-7

32-22-2-38-35-7   20-1-5-11   5-4-10   21-18-33-7:   6-1-7

4-34   8-32-15-26-35   20-1-5-11   4-29-12,   6-1-7   4-34

17-15-19-35   4-29-12   6   8-9-17-1.

2 CHRONICLES 32:24

SUDOKU
by Sara Stoker

The Philistines and the Ark

MEDIUM

	A	B	C	D	E	F	G	H	I
1		H				W		N	
2			O			G	W	H	T
3	N		G	I					
4	H			W	E			G	
5			T	H	G			I	
6			L					E	W
7	L		I		W		E	T	
8		N	W		I			L	O
9	O			G			N		

Hint: Row 1

_____ _____ kine carried the captured ark back to Israel (1 Samuel 6:12).

BIBLE QUOTATION
by Suzanne Stepp

Don't Look Back!
GENESIS 19:26

A woman's "need to know" can sometimes spice up her life a little *too* much. Work this puzzle to discover a verse about a woman whose curiosity cost her a lot.

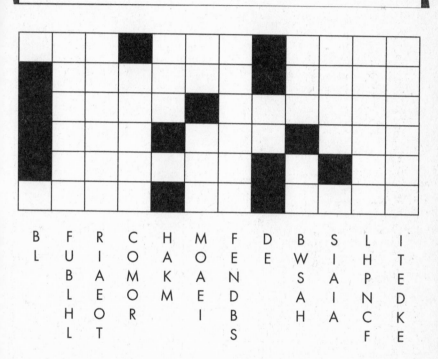

```
B  F  R  C  H  M  F  D  B  S  L  I
L  U  I  O  A  O  E  E  W  I  H  T
   B  A  M  K  A  N     S  A  P  E
   L  E  O  M  E  D     A  I  N  D
   H  O  R  I  D        H  A  C  K
      L  T        B              F  E
```

CROSSWORD
by Sarah Lagerquist Simmons

Good Guys and Villains

Isn't it great to know that good always reigns over evil? Solve this puzzle to uncover just some of the many "good guys" mentioned in the Bible, as well as the villains they came up against.

Bad guys have it in for the good guys, obsessed with doing them in. But God isn't losing any sleep; to him they're a joke with no punch line.
PSALM 37:12 MSG

ACROSS

1 American astronomer Sagan
5 "I will ____ off from the top" (Ezekiel 17:22)
9 "David took an ____, and played with his hand" (1 Samuel 16:23)
13 Healing plant included in Nicodemus's mixture (John 19:39)
14 Pundit
15 "I will even appoint over you terror, consumption, and the burning ____" (Leviticus 26:16)
16 Alpaca (var.)
17 Armor plate over the nose
18 Football six-pointer (abbr.)
19 Art technique
21 VILLAIN IN THE STORY OF MOSES
24 "Moab shall ____ over Nebo" (Isaiah 15:2)
26 "You own the cosmos. . .everything from ____ to archangel" (Psalm 89:11 MSG)
27 U.N. agency formed to defeat worldwide hunger (abbr.)
30 DAVID CUT OFF THE VILLAIN GOLIATH'S ____
32 "No decree or ____ that the king issues can be changed" (Daniel 6:15 NIV)
35 Constrained (abbr.)
36 Writer Poe
38 DAVID CUT A PIECE OF FABRIC FROM THE ____ OF A VILLAINOUS KING
40 Straighten
42 End of the day
43 VILLAIN WHO HAD JOHN THE BAPTIST KILLED

44 VILLAIN TURNED GOOD GUY
45 Ransack
47 Opposite of south-southwest (abbr.)
48 Sneer
51 Academic administrator
52 Want
53 "I have not done them of mine own ____" (Numbers 16:28)
55 Bark
57 City in northern Japan
60 VILLAINOUS RULER TO WHOM TAXES WERE DUE (Mark 12:14)
64 Girls, slang
65 Dried coconut meat
67 Weapon of war
68 "His soul shall dwell at ____" (Psalm 25:13)
69 "Let us ____ before the LORD our maker" (Psalm 95:6)
70 Gawk
71 " 'I ____ them like dirt in the streets' " (2 Samuel 22:43 NKJV)
72 "He shall ____ his angel before thee" (Genesis 24:7)
73 VILLAIN TO DAVID'S GOOD GUY

DOWN

1 The Israelites made a golden ____ to worship
2 Composed of wings
3 "Claudius had commanded all Jews to depart from ____" (Acts 18:2)
4 " 'Can you make a pet of him. . .or put him on a ____. . . ?' " (Job 41:5 NIV)
5 Woman's organization (abbr.)
6 Scrape
7 City in Nebraska

8 ALLOWED JESUS TO BE PUT TO DEATH
9 Exclamation
10 Farming (abbr.)
11 BOAZ WAS HER GOOD GUY
12 Foot (suffix)
14 Hoodwinked
20 Jewish surname from Hebrew word for priest
22 GOD USED MOSES' ____ TO PERFORM WONDERS IN FRONT OF A VILLANOUS RULER
23 Whereupon (Hung.)
25 Camp defended by wagons forming a circle
27 " 'Stand at the tent ____' " (Judges 4:20 MSG)
28 Collection of maps
29 Abhorrence
31 ____ HAD TO FLEE FOR HIS LIFE FROM SAUL
33 Trite
34 Type of steak
37 "I ____ to those whose sin does not lead to death" (1 John 5:16 NIV)
39 PARADISE WHERE THE SERPENT BEGUILED EVE

41 Glanced
43 "My lover is to me a cluster of ____ blossoms" (Song of Solomon 1:14 NIV)
46 Secular
49 "They will tear me like a lion and ____ me to pieces" (Psalm 7:2 NIV)
50 " 'Everyone who ____, has the door opened to him' " (Matthew 7:8 NLV)
54 Male honeybee
56 Exhibitions (abbr.)
57 River in France
58 SAMSON WAS ____ A GOOD GUY
59 "A man shall ____ a pit. . .and not cover it" (Exodus 21:33)
61 Chronicle
62 U.S. organization that defends individual rights (abbr.)
63 "The earth shall ____ to and fro" (Isaiah 24:20)
64 "____ thee into the land of Moriah" (Genesis 22:2)
66 THE ____ SEA WAS THE SITE OF A VILLAINOUS EGYPTIAN RULER'S DESTRUCTION

71

WORD SEARCH
by David Austin

Nathan's Parable
2 SAMUEL 12–14

And the **LORD** sent **Nathan** unto **David**. And he came unto him, and **said** unto him, There were **two men** in **one city**; the one **rich**, and the **other poor**. The rich man had **exceeding many flocks** and **herds**: But the poor man had **nothing**, save one **little ewe lamb**, which he had **bought** and **nourished** up: and it **grew** up **together** with him, and with his **children**; it did eat of his own **meat**, and **drank** of his own **cup**, and lay in his bosom, and was unto him as a **daughter**. And there came a **traveller** unto the rich man, and he **spared** to take of his own flock and of his own herd, to **dress** for the **wayfaring** man that was come unto him; but took the poor man's lamb, and dressed it for the man that was come to him.

```
D I V A D R I C H E X R T J D
E A O T E J D Q L J P O N E A
R O U H E R D S I P G O K L F
A C T G A X R E T E O P N L N
P O Z N H Z O E T H G U O B T
S M K I O T L H L H L C P R D
S U E R L U E T E W K O A Y A
E Y N A M R R R O S W V N O U
R Z M F T G N I D E E C X E G
D B E Y S N R L S L C I T Y H
E L N A E I R E L H A X E W T
N X I W M H A E W L E M H L O
T D C C A T R C H I L D R E N
D C H I L O E L L I T T W E A
J A I Q A N A H T A N E U A J
```

CRYPTOSCRIPTURE
by Donna K. Maltese

The Prophet and the Harlot

At the Lord's prompting, a prophet took to wife a harlot, an act that reflected God's displeasure with Israel's adulterous behavior. Can you break the code to discover the name of the prophet, his bride, and their firstborn son?

BJN USQ KHXN WBYN UH SHWQB, ZH,

UBIQ PJUH USQQ B GYVQ HV GSHXQNHLW

BJN FSYKNXQJ HV GSHXQNHLW: VHX USQ

KBJN SBUS FHLLYUUQN ZXQBU GSHXQNHL,

NQTBXUYJZ VXHL USQ KHXN.

IF BP EPQR DQZ RFFV YFUPN RBP ZDGYBRPN FX

ZMSADMU; EBMWB WFQWPMOPZ, DQZ SDNP

BMU D IFQ. DQZ RBP AFNZ IDMZ GQRF BMU,

WDAA BMI QDUP TPJNPPA.

SPOTTY HEADLINE

by Paul Kent and Sara Stoker

They Met Jesus

Of the billions of people who've lived on earth, only a handful actually met Jesus in the flesh. Can you solve these spotty headlines telling the stories of three men who had the great opportunity of meeting the Lord?

DEVOUT MAN RECOGNIZES BABY AS
PROMISED MESSIAH

— — — — — — —

SHORT TAX COLLECTOR HAS ZESTFULLY
RETURNED STOLEN FUNDS

— — — — — — — — —

CURIOUS PHARISEE SEEKS TOUGH
ANSWERS IN MIDDLE OF NIGHT

— — — — — — — — —

ACROSTIC
by Donna K. Maltese

A Hot Topic

Crack the code to discover the request of the rich man who found himself facing the heat "down under."

Jesus' short stories

—— —— —— —— —— —— —— ——
35 11 27 1 31 10 22 19

Hades

—— —— —— —— —— —— —— —— —— —— ——
5 28 15 3 21 34 41 13 30 24 18

Small fragment of bread

—— —— —— —— ——
39 32 20 9 14

Give witness

—— —— —— —— —— —— ——
8 40 36 23 4 12 29

What beggars have

—— —— —— ——
37 26 17 6

Lament

—— —— —— —— —— ——
25 7 16 2 33 38

12-1-15-3-2-7   1-14-30-1-3-1-9,   3-1-33-22

9-28-17-39-29   6-5   9-28,   11-5-18   19-21-5-18

10-1-37-1-34-20-36,   8-3-11-8   3-2   9-1-29   18-4-35

8-3-2   23-4-35   6-12   3-4-36   12-16-5-25-38-27   4-5

41-1-8-26-32,   11-5-18   39-6-6-24   9-29

8-13-5-25-20-40.

LUKE 16:24

CROSSWORD
by David K. Shortess

Alpha-Numeric Mix-Up

Here's a puzzle that has words and numbers mixed up in the answers to its theme clues. So get your thinking cap on, sharpen your pencils, flex your digits, and begin!

For where two or three are gathered together in my name,
there am I in the midst of them.
MATTHEW 18:20

ACROSS

1 Jehoshaphat's dad (1 Kings 15:24)
4 "Neither do they ____" (Matthew 6:28)
8 Between-meal treats
14 One Bobbsey twin
15 Ambience
16 Beach shelter
17 "He will silence her noisy ____" (Jeremiah 51:55 NIV)
18 "How we may ____ one another" (Hebrews 10:24 NIV)
19 Thomas Alva
20 JONAH'S STAY IN THE FISH (Jonah 1:17) (3 words, 2 numerals)
23 "Mine ____ is consumed with grief" (Psalm 31:9)
24 "____ the ramparts we watched"
25 Dewy
28 "____, give me this water" (John 4:15)
30 "As ____ in heaven" (Matthew 6:10) (2 words)
34 "There ____ lad here" (John 6:9) (2 words)
35 Thursday was named after him
37 "And ____ and mourning shall flee away" (Isaiah 51:11)
39 "THE FATHER, THE WORD, AND THE HOLY GHOST: ____" (1 John 5:7) (4 words, 1 numeral)
42 "Howbeit there is a kinsman ____ than I" (Ruth 3:12)
43 "And ____ it in a book" (Isaiah 30:8)
44 Contend
45 "Then came I with an ____" (Acts 23:27)
46 NUMBER OF VIRGINS WHO WENT TO MEET THE BRIDEGROOM (Matthew 25:1)

47 "A shadow from the ____" (Isaiah 25:4)
48 "Let us make ____ name" (Genesis 11:4) (2 words)
50 "As for all the hills once cultivated by the ____" (Isaiah 7:25 NIV)
52 IN WHICH THE LEAVEN WAS HIDDEN (Matthew 13:33) (3 words, 1 numeral)
61 Band leader Glenn
62 "The same shall be ____ of all" (Mark 9:35)
63 Attorneys' organization (abbr.)
64 Regal fur
65 Away from the wind and weather
66 "So a ____ tongue brings angry looks" (Proverbs 25:23 NIV)
67 Wise old man of Greek mythology
68 "Saying, What ____ these stones" (Joshua 4:21)
69 "____, of the Gentiles also" (Romans 3:29)

DOWN

1 "HE HAD ALSO SEVEN SONS ____ DAUGHTERS" (Job 42:13) (1 word, 1 numeral)
2 "And God ____, Let there be light" (Genesis 1:3)
3 "And there was one ____, a prophetess" (Luke 2:36)
4 Impudent
5 Between caterpillars and butterflies
6 "____ in the path of your commands" (Psalm 119:32 NIV) (2 words)
7 "Then Mary took about a pint of pure ____" (John 12:3 NIV)
8 "A crowd was running to the ____" (Mark 9:25 NIV)
9 Opposite the zenith

10 "He rolled _____ stone in front of the entrance" (Matthew 27:60 NIV) (2 words)
11 Country singer Johnny
12 Nautical mile per hour
13 *Lacking* or *without* (Fr.)
21 Quick affirmative
22 "THAT WHEN JEHUDI HAD READ _____ FOUR LEAVES" (Jeremiah 36:23) (1 word, 1 numeral)
25 Ephesian goddess (Acts 19:34)
26 Lou Grant: Ed _____
27 Polite address
28 Call for help
29 "Good night" girl
30 Anger
31 Word with treasure
32 Greek region where Ephesus was located
33 "Eat the fat, and drink the _____" (Nehemiah 8:10)
35 "_____ LORD is my shepherd" (Psalm 23:1)
36 "And all _____ paths are peace" (Proverbs 3:17)
37 "And _____ upon the bed" (Genesis 48:2)
38 "For _____ in the blackest darkness" (Job 28:3 NIV)
40 "But _____ the spirits whether" (1 John 4:1)

41 "AND _____ THAT SIDE" (Ezekiel 40:10) (1 word, 1 numeral)
46 "And _____ for mortar" (Genesis 11:3 NIV)
47 "And touched the _____ of his garment" (Matthew 9:20)
48 "_____ HOOKS!" (crate marking; 2 words)
49 More certain
50 Son of Beeri (Hosea 1:1)
51 "For as _____ as ye eat this bread" (1 Corinthians 11:26)
52 "BEHOLD, _____ SEEK THEE" (Acts 10:19) (1 word, 1 numeral)
53 "I sink in deep _____" (Psalm 69:2)
54 "Under oaks and poplars and _____" (Hosea 4:13)
55 Stepped down, as from a carriage
56 Shem's son (Genesis 10:22)
57 "Then let him count the years of the _____ thereof" (Leviticus 25:27)
58 "For my yoke is _____, and my burden is light" (Matthew 11:30)
59 "They say unto him, We are _____" (Matthew 20:22)
60 "The good shepherd _____ down his life for the sheep" (John 10:11 NIV)

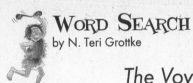

WORD SEARCH
by N. Teri Grottke

The Voyage Begins
ACTS 27:9–13

Now when much **time** was spent, and when **sailing** was now **dangerous**, because the **fast** was now **already past**, Paul **admonished** them, and said unto them, **Sirs**, I **perceive** that this **voyage** will be with **hurt** and **much damage**, not **only** of the lading and **ship**, but also of our **lives**. **Nevertheless** the **centurion believed** the **master** and the **owner** of the ship, more than those things which were **spoken** by **Paul**. And because the haven was not commodious to winter in, the more part advised to **depart** thence also, if by any **means** they might **attain** to **Phenice**, and there to winter; which is an **haven** of **Crete**, and **lieth toward** the **south west** and **north** west. And when the south wind **blew** softly, **supposing** that they had obtained their **purpose**, loosing thence, they sailed close by Crete.

```
H C U M A E S O P R U P I H S
T G N I S O P P U S N H S S Y
D F A Y C E G A Y O V E I A I
E V I E C R E P I N G N R D D
V H O N L Y E R S E D I S M A
E T I M E A U T L V R C A O N
I R L H T T S U E E A E I N G
L O W T N E A E Q R W H L I E
E N A E V P G L E T O U I S R
B I C I S A O T R H T R N H O
N W L L M T S W D E T T G E U
N E V A H A F D N L A U S D S
C L D F M S P O K E N D O A K
B B M E A N S A F S R X Y S P
R J A D E P A R T S A F C M X
```

81

ACROSTIC
by Donna K. Maltese

Redeeming Love

God loves us as Boaz loved Ruth. Solve this puzzle to discover the offer Ruth
didn't refuse from her kinsman-redeemer.

Corn

$\overline{25}$ $\overline{31}$ $\overline{5}$ $\overline{23}$ $\overline{15}$

As much as one can grasp

$\overline{16}$ $\overline{20}$ $\overline{6}$ $\overline{28}$ $\overline{10}$ $\overline{1}$ $\overline{24}$

Harvest

$\overline{33}$ $\overline{26}$ $\overline{8}$ $\overline{4}$ $\overline{19}$ $\overline{13}$

Grain used for feed, malt, and cereal (Ruth 2:17)

$\overline{11}$ $\overline{18}$ $\overline{22}$ $\overline{32}$ $\overline{3}$ $\overline{29}$

Boaz was from the _____ of Elimelech (Ruth 2:1)

$\overline{9}$ $\overline{14}$ $\overline{2}$ $\overline{30}$

Works

$\overline{27}$ $\overline{34}$ $\overline{12}$ $\overline{7}$ $\overline{21}$ $\overline{17}$

17-20-5-28   11-7-26-23   1-6-8-7   13-1-8-4,

16-3-31-21-3-17-8   8-4-7-1   6-7-8,   25-29

28-34-1-33-4-8-15-22?   33-7   6-7-8   8-7   33-27-3-18-30

5-30   2-30-7-8-4-19-13   10-5-3-32-28,   30-3-5-8-4-3-13

33-7   10-13-7-25   16-3-6-9-3,   12-1-8   20-11-5-28-19

16-3-21-3   10-2-17-8   12-29   25-29   25-2-5-28-3-6-17.

RUTH 2:8

ANAGRAM
by Paul Kent

Scenes from the Exodus

The Bible's second book is packed with memorable stories. Can you unscramble these three events from Exodus? Note: None of these exact terms is found in the King James Version, but you'll definitely recognize each one.

Go label up food

_ _ _ _ _ _   _ _

_ _ _ _ _

Throne of fat birds

_ _ _ _ _   _ _

_ _ _ _ _ _ _ _ _

Trade a spring foe

_ _ _ _ _ _ _   _ _

_ _ _   _ _ _

The Best Birthday Ever
LUKE 2:11

Solve this Bible quotation puzzle to discover the most joyous birth ever to arrive on this unstable earth.

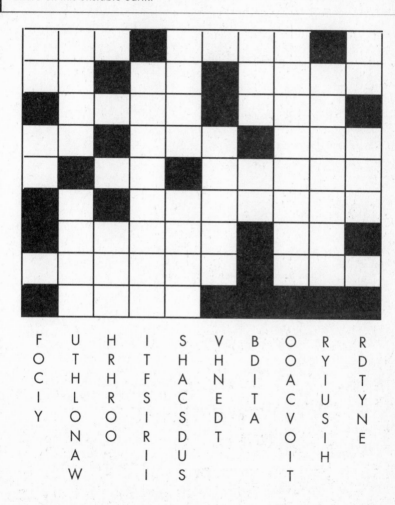

F	U	H	I	S	V	B	O	R	R
O	C	R	T	H	H	D	O	Y	D
C	H	H	F	A	N	I	A	I	T
I	L	R	S	C	E	T	C	U	Y
Y	O	O	I	S	D	A	V	S	N
	N	O	R	D	T		O	I	E
	A		I	U			I	H	
	W		I	S			T		

CROSSWORD
by Tonya Vilhauer

On Trial

To save us from sin, Jesus, an innocent man, was tried, found guilty, and condemned to die. Oh, what a Savior! As you work this puzzle, remember what He suffered for our sakes and raise up a prayer of joyful thanksgiving!

But he was wounded for our transgressions, he was bruised for our iniquities: the chastisement of our peace was upon him; and with his stripes we are healed.
ISAIAH 53:5

ACROSS

1 Cobbler (Brit.)
6 In Joseph's lineage, the son of Eliezer (Luke 3:29)
10 "Every head was made ____, and every shoulder was peeled" (Ezekiel 29:18)
14 Diamond weight unit
15 Black (var.)
16 A dueling sword
17 Impersonation
18 A SOLDIER PIERCED JESUS' ____. (John 19:34)
19 Praise
20 Plateau
21 Prompt
22 "The vessel that he made of clay was ____" (Jeremiah 18:4)
24 Slant
26 HE SAID, "I FIND NO FAULT IN THIS MAN" (Luke 23:4)
27 Loose
30 Flow out slowly
31 Relating to hearing
32 "A ____ word stirs up anger" (Proverbs 15:1 NIV)
33 Radio frequency band (abbr.)
36 "SAVE THYSELF, AND COME DOWN FROM THE ____" (Mark 15:30)
37 "They would have repented long ____ in sackcloth and ashes" (Matthew 11:21)
38 "Thou shalt not ____ carnally with thy neighbour's wife" (Leviticus 18:20)
39 Compass point (abbr.)
40 "Ye blind guides, which strain at a ____, and swallow a camel" (Matthew 23:24)
41 Moisten meat
43 Cowboy apparel

44 "Thou shalt utterly ____ it, and thou shalt utterly abhor it" (Deuteronomy 7:26)
45 Stomach muscles (abbr.)
48 "For God ____ love" (1 John 4:8)
49 Invoke
50 Raise higher
51 "It shall be seven days under the ____" (Leviticus 22:27)
52 "For there shall be no ____ of any man's life" (Acts 27:22)
56 "Expose these things for the ____ they are" (Ephesians 5:11 MSG)
57 Private school (abbr.)
59 Church part
60 Antic
61 "The greater light to ____ the day" (Genesis 1:16)
62 "You are from ____; I am from above" (John 8:23 NIV)
63 "Is this house, which is called by my name, become ____ of robbers?" (Jeremiah 7:11) (2 words)
64 "AND THEY ____ UPON HIM. . .AND SMOTE HIM" (Matthew 27:30)
65 THEY PUT A ____ OF THORNS ON JESUS' HEAD (Matthew 27:29)

DOWN

1 "I worked an elaborate ____? Where's the evidence?" (2 Corinthians 12:16–17 MSG)
2 "She took the goatskins and covered. . . the smooth ____ of his neck" (Genesis 27:15 MSG)
3 Minerals
4 "WHOM WILL YE THAT I RELEASE UNTO YOU? ____, OR JESUS. . .?" (Matthew 27:17)

5 Pigpen
6 "BUT ____ HELD HIS PEACE" (Matthew 26:63)
7 Off-Broadway award
8 "And Jacob ____ pottage" (Genesis 25:29)
9 "Love your ____, do good to them which hate you" (Luke 6:27)
10 Baseball player Yogi
11 "Wherefore lay ____ all filthiness" (James 1:21)
12 Embankment
13 "If we. . .be examined of the good ____ done" (Acts 4:9)
21 Key
23 A to Z
25 "They are not plagued by human ____" (Psalm 73:5 NIV)
26 Philanthropist and former presidential contender
27 Women's branch of U.S. Army in World War II (abbr.)
28 "Let us kill him, that the inheritance may be ____" (Luke 20:14)
29 "Led him unto the ____ of the hill" (Luke 4:29)
30 Epics
32 "PILATE. . .WASHED HIS ____ BEFORE THE MULTITUDE" (Matthew 27:24)

33 "Thy life be for his life, or ____ thou shalt pay a talent of silver" (1 Kings 20:39)
34 "The sword that ____ him cannot cut" (Job 41:26 NLV)
35 "BEHOLD MY HANDS AND MY ____" (Luke 24:39)
40 Acoustical or electric stringed instruments
42 Artist's studio
44 "Now the eyes of Israel were ____ for age" (Genesis 48:10)
45 Ladybug fare
46 "First the ____, then the ear, after that the full corn" (Mark 4:28)
47 HE CARRIED JESUS' CROSS (Matthew 27:32)
49 Plebe
50 Beef graders (abbr.)
51 Surrealist Spanish painter
53 Scandinavian national capital
54 "The LORD is. . .____ to anger" (Psalm 103:8)
55 Stitched together
58 "LET THIS ____ PASS FROM ME" (Matthew 26:39)
59 TV network (abbr.)

87

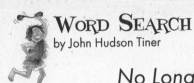

WORD SEARCH
by John Hudson Tiner

No Longer Doubting
JOHN 20:26–28

And **after eight days again** his **disciples** were **within**, and **Thomas** with **them**: then **came Jesus**, the **doors being shut**, and **stood** in the **midst**, and said, **Peace** be unto you. **Then saith** he to Thomas, Reach hither thy **finger**, and **behold** my **hands**; and **reach hither** thy hand, and **thrust** it into my **side**: and be not **faithless**, but **believing**. And Thomas **answered** and said unto him, My **Lord** and my God.

```
S A M O H T L U D B D A Y S H
E S I D E H P H L E Z O K L A
L M E H T K C K O O C H O O N
P A Q L P F A A H B C A K R D
I Q N J H F G N E H T B E D S
C G W S A T A L B R H G C P F
S W I K W E I G H T N S O W A
I F T T B E N A H I T H E R U
D M H E V W R T F O S S R S E
T J I I Y Y I E O C U R Y O M
P N N D V A V D D S R E T F A
G G Q N S H C H E R H C U G C
W F V H U T E J G F T Y H I Y
M N C E A F U E N I E B S N M
E S D G H A E T A V T L E Q D
```

Drop Two

by Dorothy Pryse

Peter Jailed
See Acts 12:5

Herod hated people who worshiped Jesus. Work this drop two puzzle to discover what this king did to sabotage Peter's influence on his people.

STRANGE	Bestow	_____	1. ___ ___
OCTOPUS	Boy or girl	_____	2. ___ ___
PETRIFY	Torridly hot	_____	3. ___ ___
EROSIVE	Wanders	_____	4. ___ ___
TRODDEN	More peculiar	_____	5. ___ ___
POWDERY	Bride's offering	_____	6. ___ ___
SPARRED	Shovel	_____	7. ___ ___
WARSHIP	Key signature	_____	8. ___ ___
SESTINA	Beer mug	_____	9. ___ ___
SEAPORT	Talk idly	_____	10. ___ ___
NORFOLK	Level surface	_____	11. ___ ___

— — — — — — — — — — —

1 2 3 4 5 6 7 8 9 10 11

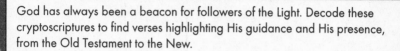

To Show the Way

God has always been a beacon for followers of the Light. Decode these
cryptoscriptures to find verses highlighting His guidance and His presence,
from the Old Testament to the New.

KYZ WCR UQBZ NRYW XRAQBR WCRI XV ZKV

MY K JMUUKB QA K EUQDZ, WQ URKZ WCRI

WCR NKV; KYZ XV YMTCW MY K JMUUKB QA

AMBR, WQ TMSR WCRI UMTCW; WQ TQ XV

ZKV KYZ YMTCW.

HGK AIB AIHEE UZVGY OTZPI H ATG, HGK PITJ

AIHEP SHEE IVA GHQB MBAJA: OTZ IB AIHEE

AHWB IVA LBTLEB OZTQ PIBVZ AVGA.

ACROSTIC
by Donna K. Maltese

A Bewitching Tale

Solve the puzzle to discover the tale of a man who dabbled in magic and, for a spell, developed quite a following.

He converted an Ethiopian eunuch (Acts 8:26–38)

$\overline{22}$ $\overline{8}$ $\overline{31}$ $\overline{26}$ $\overline{2}$ $\overline{15}$

Caster of spells

$\overline{13}$ $\overline{27}$ $\overline{7}$ $\overline{3}$ $\overline{20}$

Skill in deceiving to gain something

$\overline{23}$ $\overline{9}$ $\overline{1}$ $\overline{17}$ $\overline{12}$

Satan's henchmen

$\overline{18}$ $\overline{11}$ $\overline{28}$ $\overline{30}$ $\overline{21}$ $\overline{5}$

Make confused

$\overline{14}$ $\overline{29}$ $\overline{6}$ $\overline{25}$ $\overline{19}$ $\overline{4}$

Clever

$\overline{16}$ $\overline{10}$ $\overline{24}$

7-8-4-9-4   13-1-5   1   23-29-9-12-1-27-21   28-1-21,

23-1-10-10-29-18   19-31-28-30-21,   13-20-2-3-20

14-11-17-30-9-11-12-2-6-11   2-21   7-8-4   16-1-6-29

23-2-12-24   25-5-29-18   19-30-9-3-29-9-24,   1-21-18

14-11-13-2-12-3-20-11-18   7-8-4   15-11-30-22-26-11

30-17   16-1-6-1-9-2-1.

ACTS 8:9

CROSSWORD
by David K. Shortess

Biblical Big Boys

Because the Lord is with us, we need not fear anything—no matter how gigantic. Solve this puzzle to uncover verses dealing with biblical big boys who lived in days of yore.

And there we saw the giants. . .and we were in our own sight as grasshoppers, and so we were in their sight.
NUMBERS 13:33

ACROSS

1 Its capital has been Agana
5 "In ____ also is his tabernacle" (Psalm 76:2)
10 "And he ____ the sin of many" (Isaiah 53:12)
14 Taj Mahal city
15 North Florida city
16 Son of Seth (Genesis 4:26)
17 "____ IN THE EARTH IN THOSE DAYS" (Genesis 6:4) (3 words)
20 Help a felon
21 *Dead*, in Paris
22 "Surely in vain the ____ is spread" (Proverbs 1:17)
25 "And they filled them up to the ____" (John 2:7)
27 In abundance
31 "And ____ of oil" (Leviticus 14:21) (2 words)
33 Company head
35 "Able was I ____ saw Elba" (2 words)
36 Slightest
39 Home of the Mets
42 Japanese volcano
43 "THERE WENT OUT A CHAMPION. . . NAMED ____, WHOSE HEIGHT WAS SIX CUBITS AND A SPAN" (1 Samuel 17:4) (3 words)
46 Pale
47 Malayan sailboat (var.)
48 Treble clef guys
50 "The ____ are a people not strong" (Proverbs 30:25)
52 Swift boat from Vietnam War (abbr.)
54 Three in Thüringen
55 Put away

58 Kind of hoop
61 1,760 equal 1 mi. (abbr.)
62 "He. . .measured the ____ all around" (Ezekiel 42:15 NIV)
64 "How much ____ shall I answer him" (Job 9:14)
66 "WITH ALL BASHAN, WHICH WAS CALLED ____" (Deuteronomy 3:13) (4 words)
73 "Wherein I ____ erred" (Job 6:24)
74 Tapeworm (var.)
75 "____ certain man was sick" (John 11:1) (2 words)
76 "And Abraham lifted up his ____" (Genesis 22:13)
77 Fishhook leader
78 "The nations are as a ____ of a bucket" (Isaiah 40:15)

DOWN

1 "And Moses ____ him into the camp" (Numbers 11:30)
2 Cry of disgust
3 "____ not my days few" (Job 10:20)
4 "Call me not Naomi, call me ____" (Ruth 1:20)
5 "Hear ye therefore the parable of the ____" (Matthew 13:18)
6 Acid found in vinegar
7 Roman household god or spirit
8 Primary school (abbr.)
9 "And I will send a fire on ____" (Ezekiel 39:6)
10 George Harrison was one
11 New England Cape
12 "But the name of the wicked shall ____" (Proverbs 10:7)

13 Ogee shape

18 "As their lives ____ away in their mothers' arms" (Lamentations 2:12 NIV)

19 "Was ____ the son of Ikkesh" (1 Chronicles 27:9)

22 Viet ____

23 Appealing to refined taste

24 Blue Jays' home

26 Furnace survivor (Daniel 3:26)

28 Public speaking

29 Tear up again

30 Old MacDonald's refrain ending

32 Hair goop

34 Expression of discovery

37 A little drink

38 "Now the Valley of Siddim was full of ____ pits" (Genesis 14:10 NIV)

40 Newt

41 "He is of ____; ask him" (John 9:23)

44 "From the ____ of the rocks I see him" (Numbers 23:9)

45 "____ the Word was made flesh" (John 1:14)

46 "There ____ a man sent from God" (John 1:6)

49 Bro's sib

51 Marshlands

53 "I am not come to destroy, but to ____" (Matthew 5:17)

56 Baseball stat

57 Fender blemishes

59 "It must be settled in a ____ assembly" (Acts 19:39 NIV)

60 "As many ____ love, I rebuke and chasten" (Revelation 3:19) (2 words)

63 "Ye have made it ____ of thieves" (Luke 19:46) (2 words)

65 "I shall multiply my days as the ____" (Job 29:18)

66 "____ LORD is my light" (Psalm 27:1)

67 "The ____ is withered away" (Isaiah 15:6)

68 "Adam was. . .formed, then ____" (1 Timothy 2:13)

69 "I am ____ that bear witness of myself" (John 8:18)

70 "Fight neither with small ____ great" (1 Kings 22:31)

71 "No man can serve ____ masters" (Matthew 6:24)

72 "The trees. . .are full of ____" (Psalm 104:16)

TELEPHONE SCRAMBLE
by Nancy Bernhard and Connie Troyer

Cursed

Here are things, places, people, and objects that were the opposite of blessed, some through no fault of their own. Can you solve the puzzle to figure them out?

ABC 2	ABC 2	GHI 4	MNO 6

ABC 2	ABC 2	MNO 6	ABC 2	ABC 2	MNO 6

GHI 4	PRS 7	MNO 6	TUV 8	MNO 6	DEF 3

MNO 6	ABC 2	TUV 8	TUV 8	PRS 7	DEF 3

PRS 7	DEF 3	PRS 7	PRS 7	DEF 3	MNO 6	TUV 8

JKL 5	TUV 8	DEF 3	ABC 2	GHI 4

Jezebel's Death

MEDIUM

	A	B	C	D	E	F	G	H	I
1			W				O		H
2		S		A		O			R
3	A		O	W				S	
4	R							T	S
5			H		S	W			
6		A	I			H	R	O	
7	I			S	D		A		
8									T
9	T	O	A			R	S		D

Hint: Row 6

"And he _____, _____ her down. So they threw her down: and some of her blood was sprinkled on the wall, and on the horses: and he trode her under foot" (2 Kings 9:33).

Word Search
by David Austin

Sodom and Gomorrah
GENESIS 19:24–28

Then the **Lord rained** upon **Sodom** and upon **Gomorrah brimstone** and **fire** from the Lord out of **heaven**; and he **overthrew** those **cities**, and all the **plain**, and all the **inhabitants** of the cities, and that which **grew** upon the **ground**. But his **wife looked back** from **behind** him, and she **became** a **pillar** of **salt**. And **Abraham** gat up **early** in the **morning** to the **place** where he **stood** before the Lord: And he looked toward Sodom and Gomorrah, and toward all the **land** of the plain, and beheld, and, lo, the **smoke** of the **country** went up as the smoke of a **furnace**.

```
B  X  B  R  A  I  N  E  D  O  O  T  S  A  P
I  T  L  A  N  D  R  G  R  O  U  N  D  J  N
Q  J  P  L  C  I  A  N  B  V  W  I  F  E  P
K  L  C  L  F  K  Y  X  H  E  N  N  V  P  Z
Z  G  N  I  N  R  O  M  W  R  C  A  H  L  L
W  U  E  P  T  S  W  O  Y  T  E  A  L  A  W
L  S  T  N  A  T  I  B  A  H  N  I  M  C  B
L  L  U  L  O  O  K  E  D  R  P  Z  W  E  L
E  O  T  X  R  T  L  A  S  E  Q  L  Y  S  B
C  R  R  G  E  U  S  M  B  W  N  L  A  E  R
A  H  A  D  G  G  O  M  O  R  R  A  H  I  K
N  Y  L  T  R  K  F  O  I  A  A  I  C  T  N
R  D  R  U  E  R  S  D  E  R  N  H  E  I  D
U  B  N  W  W  U  E  O  E  D  B  A  A  C  J
F  A  I  Q  A  U  U  S  M  Z  P  P  G  M  A
```

ACROSTIC
by Donna K. Maltese

One Great Catch

When we listen to Jesus, we reap great benefits. Solve this puzzle to discover how some fishermen were blessed with bounty after heeding Jesus' advice.

The sea on which this story takes place (John 21:1)

___ ___ ___ ___ ___ ___ ___ ___
21 36 15 3   41 11 28 33

Simon and Andrew's initial livelihood (Matthew 4:18)

___ ___ ___ ___ ___ ___ ___ ___ ___
8   14 22 40 34 27 2   19 12

The disciples followed Jesus' ____ (John 21:6)

___ ___ ___ ___ ___ ___ ___ ___ ___
1   23 10 29 35 7   13 20 31

The apostle who took a dive (John 21:7)

___ ___ ___ ___ ___
16 42 30 24 18

The night before, the disciples ____ naught (John 21:3)

___ ___ ___ ___ ___ ___
39 4   25 17 5   37

If we ____ depend on Jesus, we will have more than enough

___ ___ ___ ___ ___ ___
43 38 6   32 9   26

35-4-22-7 7-5-3 12-3-30 6-12 7-5-3 18-23-17-5-37

33-14-1-3 6-8 7-5-3 33-5-36-16, 4-31-1 26-42

33-40-28-9-9 8-11-12-1. 7-5-3-26 39-4-22-7

7-5-3-10-3-8-20-10-3, 4-31-1 12-6-43 7-5-3-26

43-24-41-24 12-6-21 28-15-9-34 7-6 1-27-4-43

13-7 8-20-10 7-5-3 2-25-32-7-13-7-25-1-29 20-8

8-11-22-38-19-22.

JOHN 21:6

SPOTTY HEADLINE
by Paul Kent and Sara Stoker

Ruined Lives

"Choose life," God commanded His people through Moses. But not everyone chooses wisely. These spotty headlines relate to the stories of three men who blew it, big-time. Can you solve them?

●EBREW SL●IN FOR SN●TCHING JERI●HO PLU●DER

— — — — —

DECEPTIO● COME● B●CK TO H●UNT CHR●STI●N BE●EFACTOR

— — — — — —

UN●UST ●INFUL MAN COMMITS S●ICI●E RATHER THAN ●SK FORGIVENESS

— — — — —

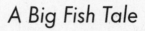

A Big Fish Tale

When God calls us to perform a duty, we would be wise to stop treading water and swim in His will.

1. SUSJE

2. RWOSD

3. HNREET

4. ELTNMA

5. AHHPROA

6. TWDLE

7. TTLHWFE

8. NLAIS

9. EANLFL

10. TUDETMLIU

Jesus made reference to this slimy story.

1. ◯ _ _ _ _

2. _ _ ◯ _ _

3. ◯ _ _ _ _ _

4. _ ◯ _ _ _ _

5. _ _ _ _ _ _ ◯

6. _ ◯ _ _ _

7. _ _ _ _ _ _ ◯

8. _ _ ◯ _ _

9. _ _ _ ◯ _ _

10. _ _ _ _ _ _ _ _ ◯

Answer: _ _ _ _ _ _ and the _ _ _ _ _

CROSSWORD
by Tonya Vilhauer

A Double Portion

Sometimes good things come in twos, as in the case of the godly men revealed in this puzzle. Pay "pair-ticular" attention to the clues when teaming up these faithful and honorable duos. . . .

Let the elders that rule well be counted worthy of double honour.
1 TIMOTHY 5:17

ACROSS

1 Whipped dairy food
6 Madagascar franc (abbr.)
9 RED-HAIRED TWIN (Genesis 25:25)
13 Shampoo brand
14 To suffer illness
15 "Ahasuerus laid a tribute. . .upon the ____ of the sea" (Esther 10:1)
16 Colder
17 One (Sp.)
18 "They look and ____ upon me" (Psalm 22:17)
19 ____ vu
20 "THE SPIRIT OF ELIJAH DOTH REST ON ____" (2 Kings 2:15)
22 Up-to-date (abbr.)
23 Amendment proposed to guarantee equal rights regardless of sex (abbr.)
24 Time zone (abbr.)
25 "The coat was without ____" (John 19:23)
27 "Take thee a ____ knife" (Ezekiel 5:1)
29 Spanish fortress commander
33 Outlaw
34 "I have broken the ____ of Pharaoh" (Ezekiel 30:21)
35 Christmas carol
36 HEEL-HOLDING TWIN (Genesis 25:26)
39 Swollen spot on the eyelid
40 "His spear ____ in the ground" (1 Samuel 26:7)
41 Seaweed substance
42 Roberto's "Yes!"
43 "They were ____ filled with the Holy Ghost" (Acts 2:4)
44 "JACOB GAVE ESAU BREAD AND ____" (Genesis 25:34)
46 "Your own ____ have said" (Acts 17:28)
49 Father
50 Compass point (abbr.)
51 "Given to hospitality, ____ to teach" (1 Timothy 3:2)
53 Crow's cry
56 Assign
58 Soft cheese
59 Red pigment (var.)
61 Native or resident of (suffix)
62 Fish tank dweller
63 "The first day of the feast of unleavened ____ the disciples came to Jesus" (Matthew 26:17)
64 Pastor (abbr.)
65 Step
66 "Let the archer ____ his bow" (Jeremiah 51:3)
67 Compass point (abbr.)
68 Celebration

DOWN

1 "He will not always ____: neither. . . keep his anger" (Psalm 103:9)
2 Speed contestants
3 ELISHA BECAME HIS SERVANT (1 Kings 19:21)
4 Adrift
5 "After this manner will I ____ the pride of Judah" (Jeremiah 13:9)
6 Pilate said he found no ____ in this man (Luke 23:4)

7 Brief

8 List of definitions

9 Suffix denoting the most

10 Close the door hard

11 Air (prefix)

12 "The ox hath _____ to push in time past" (Exodus 21:36)

15 JACOB AND ESAU'S FATHER (Genesis 25:26)

20 Cable sports channel

21 Great ships can be turned by a very small _____ (James 3:4)

24 *The Little Mermaid*'s Sebastian

26 ELISHA TOOK ELIJAH'S _____ (2 Kings 2:13)

28 Terminates

30 Note of debt

31 Last month of year (abbr.)

32 Deer relative

34 Snacked

36 Native of Nippon (abbr.)

37 "I knew a man in Christ above fourteen years _____" (2 Corinthians 12:2)

38 Kitty

39 Dozers

40 "The Cretians are alway liars, evil beasts, _____ bellies" (Titus 1:12)

42 Giant

43 Church part

45 Helped

47 What dentists remove

48 ELISHA ASKED FOR A DOUBLE PORTION OF ELIJAH'S _____ (2 Kings 2:9)

50 Actor Martin

52 Watery

53 Baseball player Ty

54 "As it were a half _____ of land" (1 Samuel 14:14)

55 "And _____ the day of Pentecost was fully come" (Acts 2:1)

57 "Learn to maintain good works for necessary _____" (Titus 3:14)

58 Second letter of the Greek alphabet

60 Radiation dose (abbr.)

62 Cooking measurement (abbr.)

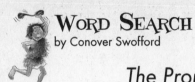

WORD SEARCH
by Conover Swofford

The Promised Land

ABRAHAM	MIGHTY MEN
ACHAN	MILK
ALTAR	MOSES
ARK	POMEGRANATES
CANAAN	PRIEST
GIANTS	RAHAB
GIBEON	SPY
GRAPES	STONES
HONEY	TRIBES
ISRAEL	VALOR
JORDAN	WAR
JOSHUA	

```
G T J U L O P A Q X Z Y T T R
G J O Q C A N A A N P H R S N
I P P X Z B H T S T O N E S S
B R R S P R I E S T M S R R R
E C L B J A W C S R E H R A R
O Y E N O H A R T I G L T V L
N B Y B R A R K N B R L X A S
I A Y Y D M E E A E A Y Y L T
T U R P A E M R D S N H A O N
E H T T N Y P N N A M A R A
S S R S T R S R E S T R S R I
K O G H G R R S C S E P A R G
L J G A C H A N S Z S E Y P S
I I S R A E L X E Z E C C R G
M O S E S T T X D A H A R R G
```

ACROSTIC
by Donna K. Maltese

Talk about Job Loss!

When bereft of all his worldly goods, Job still maintained a good attitude.
Solve this puzzle to find out his exact frame of mind.

Job was God's _____ (Job 1:8)

—— —— —— —— —— —— ——
13 34 28 23 1 18 9

God's protection (Job 1:10)

—— —— —— —— ——
24 17 5 31 12

Calamity

—— —— —— —— —— —— —— —— —— ——
11 26 2 19 8 22 29 4 32 36

Dismal

—— —— —— —— ——
6 20 14 33 27

God let Satan have his _____ with Job

—— —— ——
30 15 3

In all his suffering, Job never _____ God

—— —— —— —— —— ——
35 25 10 21 7 16

18-33-27-17-16   35-15-11-34   26   8-25-29   8-19

11-3   11-8-29-24-7-28-2   30-8-11-6,   1-32-5

18-33-27-17-16   13-24-15-20-20   26   22-36-29-4-22-18

9-24-26-9-24-7-10:   9-24-7   20-8-10-5   31-15-23-14,

1-32-5   9-24-7   20-8-10-5   24-15-9-24   9-15-27-7-18

1-30-1-3;   6-20-12-21-21-12-16   6-12   9-24-7

18-33-11-17   8-19   9-24-7   20-8-10-5.

JOB 1:21

ANAGRAM
by Paul Kent

Jesus Was Here

Stories of Jesus are the best stories imaginable. Can you unscramble these three events in the Lord's life? Note: None of these exact terms is found in the King James Version, but you'll definitely know them and their stories.

Puts pearls

__ __ __ __   __ __ __ __ __ __

Fast rain touring

__ __ __ __ __ __ __ __ __ __ __ __ __ __ __

As in cones

__ __ __ __ __ __ __ __

Zechariah's Seventh Vision

This prophet wasn't horsing around when he experienced his seventh vision. Can you break the cryptoscripture codes to discover the vehicles seen and what they represented?

YCR H OQKCPR, YCR BHNOPR QG AHCP

PVPM, YCR BEEDPR, YCR, ZPJEBR, OJPKP TYAP

NEQK TJYKHEOM EQO NKEA ZPOXPPC OXE

AEQCOYHCM; YCR OJP AEQCOYHCM XPKP

AEQCOYHCM EN ZKYMM.

DAQ UYC DARCP DAXBCZCQ DAQ XDTQ OAUH

LC, UYCXC DZC UYC GHOZ XNTZTUX HG UYC

YCDMCAX, BYTJY RH GHZUY GZHL XUDAQTAR

FCGHZC UYC PHZQ HG DPP UYC CDZUY.

CROSSWORD
by David K. Shortess

Sowing the Word

To reap a bountiful harvest for Christ, we must not only be grounded in the Word, but obey, serve, and persist in the Way, keeping our eyes on Jesus. Field these scriptural clues to find a crop of "sow-ful" answers scattered throughout this puzzle.

Hearken; Behold, there went out a sower to sow:
And it came to pass, as he sowed. . .
MARK 4:3–4

ACROSS

1. "Who ____ thou?" (Genesis 27:32)
4. "____ a watch, O LORD" (Psalm 141:3)
7. "How right they are to ____ you!" (Song of Solomon 1:4 NIV)
12. Constrictors
14. Japheth's father (Genesis 5:32)
15. "No mention shall be made of ____" (Job 28:18)
16. Ambience
17. "There is none ____" (Deuteronomy 4:39)
18. Short news pieces
19. "SOME FELL ____" (Mark 4:4) (4 words)
22. One who stores fodder on a farm
23. Lots of ounces (abbr.)
24. Its agents work underground (abbr.)
27. Repeat in music
28. Used in posting a letter to oneself
29. "And it became ____ in his hand" (Exodus 4:4) (2 words)
30. Naval initials
33. "And some fell on ____ " (Mark 4:5) (2 words)
36. Indian princess or rajah's wife
38. "Have gone into exile, captive before the ____" (Lamentations 1:5 NIV)
39. It may be a golden one
40. "AND SOME FELL ____ " (Mark 4:7) (2 words)
43. "Doth not the ____ try words?" (Job 12:11)
44. "And cried with a ____ voice" (Mark 5:7)
45. "To ____, Jerusalem" (Jeremiah 25:18)
46. "Which strain ____ gnat" (Matthew 23:24) (2 words)
48. "And it ____ upon each of them" (Acts 2:3)
49. Brother's sibling (abbr.)
50. "Even on the ____ laid a very heavy yoke" (Isaiah 47:6 NIV) (2 words)
54. "AND OTHER FELL ____ " (Mark 4:8) (3 words)
56. "Let me ____" (Deuteronomy 9:14)
59. "But thou art ____" (Daniel 4:18)
60. Son of Boaz (Ruth 4:21)
61. Sweet, musically (Ital.)
62. Homophone for land amphibian
63. "And mules, a ____ year by year" (2 Chronicles 9:24)
64. More strange
65. "And the moon shall not give ____ light" (Ezekiel 32:7)
66. "Let them not feed, ____ drink water" (Jonah 3:7)

DOWN

1. "For he is ____ " (Hebrews 5:13) (2 words)
2. City in southwest Quebec
3. Small pies
4. Free energy?
5. "For my yoke is ____" (Matthew 11:30)
6. "Then shall ____ return" (Joshua 20:6) (2 words)
7. Sulfuric and nitric
8. "And they shall ____" (Jeremiah 50:36)
9. "And my people the ____" (Jeremiah 6:27 NIV)

10 "And a _____ on every altar" (Numbers 23:30)

11 Golfer Ernie

13 Indian honorific

14 Latest

20 Pillar in Wales

21 "_____ you, don't torture me!" (Luke 8:28 NIV) (2 words)

24 Indecorous

25 Western Turkey, at one time

26 "By the way, an _____ in the path" (Genesis 49:17)

28 Snob

29 Popular ISP (abbr.)

30 They separate Asia from Europe

31 Apia location

32 "As a jewel of gold in a swine's _____" (Proverbs 11:22)

34 "Abraham, and _____ unto Isaac" (1 Chronicles 16:16) (3 words)

35 List of names

37 "Nor _____ of life" (Hebrews 7:3)

41 "Away like a _____ on the surface of the waters" (Hosea 10:7 NIV)

42 Griped and whined

47 "I had digged in the wall, behold _____ " (Ezekiel 8:8) (2 words)

49 "At whom do you _____ and stick out your tongue?" (Isaiah 57:4 NIV)

50 Psychiatrist who rejected Freud

51 Coffee type

52 "Every _____ his brother" (Jeremiah 34:17) (2 words)

53 Milk faucet

54 "Saying, Come up this _____" (Judges 16:18)

55 Bassoon relative

56 "Why make ye this _____, and weep?" (Mark 5:39)

57 "The children of _____" (Nehemiah 7:37)

58 "I am an _____ man" (Luke 1:18)

WORD SEARCH
by David Austin

The Betrayer

BETRAY
CHIEF PRIESTS
CONDEMNED
CONSPIRE
COVENANTED
DELIVER
DISCIPLE
ELDERS
GETHSEMANE
HANGED
ISCARIOT
JUDAS
KISS
MASTER
MULTITUDE

OPPORTUNITY
PHARISEES
PIECES
REPENTED
SCRIBES
SIGN
SILVER
SIMON'S SON
SINNED
THIEF
THIRTY
TORCHES
TRAITOR
TRANSGRESSION
WEAPONS

```
B E T R A Y S I N N E D B X A
P P I E C E S E L P I C S I D
I I W T T H A N G E D O J Q E
S E E S I R A H P E P V J E L
C C A A T P A K N P N E T D I
A O P M P S I M O K L N O U V
R N O I S S E R G S N A R T E
I S N C S D T I I X H N C I R
O P S N N U E M R E N T H T E
T I Z O N Z O T T P L E E L V
N R C I W N H L N H F D S U L
G E T H S E M A N E I E E M I
I Y W S E B I R C S P R I R S
S R O T I A R T J D A E T H S
Y N J U D A S T H I E F R Y C
```

BIBLE QUOTATION
by Suzanne Stepp

Answered Prayer
1 SAMUEL 1:20

If we pray in faith, we will receive in faith. Solve this puzzle to discover the woman who got what she asked for and then gave it back.

S	W	C	B	D	E	T	V	A	C	R	E
E	L	H	S	M	V	A	I	T	D	A	A
T	A	O	R	D	M	U	H	R	H	E	E
T	I	N	H	A	E	U	C	O	A	O	A
Y	E	H	I	O	W	O	E	S	D	P	M
M	L	A	E	S	E	H	T	A	F	S	I
D	I	M	S	C	N	E	S	L	H	K	E
A	S	T	A	N	E	I	A	B	E	N	C
H	A	O	N	A	U	E	O	A	T	H	A
R	C	H	E	O	N	A	F	E	S	S	T
	I	L	W	M	H	N		N	U		E
			G	H	B	F					D
			A								E
			E								

116

TELEPHONE SCRAMBLE

by Nancy Bernhard and Connie Troyer

Allegories

Some things are used as a symbolic representation of a hidden truth. Can you solve this puzzle to uncover some of these allegorical people, animals, places, and things?

GHI 4	ABC 2	GHI 4	ABC 2	PRS 7

JKL 5	GHI 4	MNO 6	MNO 6	DEF 3	PRS 7	PRS 7

PRS 7	ABC 2	PRS 7	ABC 2	GHI 4

TUV 8	GHI 4	MNO 6	DEF 3

TUV 8	GHI 4	MNO 6	DEF 3	WXY 9	ABC 2	PRS 7	DEF 3

GHI 4	MNO 6	MNO 6	DEF 3	PRS 7

ACROSTIC
by Donna K. Maltese

A Hair-Razing Tale

Crack the code to discover the ploy a calculating woman used to cut down a mighty Nazarite.

Delilah was hired by lords of the _____ (Judges 16:5)

___ ___ ___ ___ ___ ___ ___ ___ ___ ___ ___
15   3   12 24   5   21 34 31   9   28   8

Delilah wove Samson's locks with this (Judges 16:13)

___ ___ ___
29   2   17

Samson's father (Judges 13:20–24)

___ ___ ___ ___ ___ ___
16 33 19 11   1   22

To calculate

___ ___ ___ ___ ___ ___
23   4   30 10 18   27

How often Delilah nagged Samson (Judges 16:16)

___ ___ ___ ___ ___
32 26 13   7   20

To shear

___ ___ ___
25 14   6

32-27-24-5-24-33-22 21-26-12-32 34-11

8-1-16-8-11-19, 34-2-7-7 16-2, 5 15-18-1-20

6-3-2-2, 29-3-2-18-2-31-19 6-3-20 30-18-28-1-34

21-34-18-27-9-30-34-22 7-13-28-34-22, 1-9-32

29-3-2-18-2-29-4-6-3 6-3-11-14 16-4-30-3-6-27-8-6

17-2 17-11-10-19-32 34-11 1-23-23-7-4-25-34

6-3-2-2.

JUDGES 16:6

CROSSWORD
by Tonya Vilhauer

Overcomers

When God is with us, we can overcome any obstacles that cross our paths. Work this puzzle to discover biblical men who, with help from above, lived victorious lives.

*Ye are of God, little children, and have overcome them:
because greater is he that is in you, than he that is in the world.*
1 JOHN 4:4

ACROSS

1 Agency charged with protecting the environment (abbr.)
4 "I'll. . .____ your bones in the valleys" (Ezekiel 32:5 MSG)
9 "And none ____ stay his hand" (Daniel 4:35)
12 "Till they ____ the stone from the well's mouth" (Genesis 29:8)
14 Speak in public
15 "He that findeth his life shall ____ it" (Matthew 10:39)
16 WHERE PAUL WAS HELD PRISONER IN ACTS 28:16
17 Helmet's nosepiece
18 Colored part of eye
19 OTHERWISE KNOWN AS HANANIAH (Daniel 1:7)
21 Behold (2 words)
23 Wrath
24 ____ Fran.
25 On the foot of cat or dog
28 DANIEL'S "FRIENDLY" HOME (Daniel 6:16)
31 Invitation abbreviation
34 ROYAL ADVISOR TO NEBUCHADNEZZAR, BELSHAZZAR, AND DARIUS
36 Teachers' labor union (abbr.)
38 French "yes"
40 "The Pharisees began to ____ him vehemently" (Luke 11:53)
41 To incorporate
43 Tenor
44 Stretch to make do
45 African antelope
46 Time periods

48 "And shall ____ carry captives into Egypt" (Daniel 11:8)
51 "That I may ____ Christ" (Philippians 3:8)
53 "That they might not ____ thy voice" (Daniel 9:11)
54 Hertz (abbr.)
56 "The king of the south. . .shall return into his ____ land" (Daniel 11:9)
58 Detective
61 OTHERWISE KNOWN AS AZARIAH (Daniel 1:7)
66 Title of peerage
67 "Thou art a stranger, and also an ____" (2 Samuel 15:19)
69 "The king of Babylon will stop. . .to seek an ____" (Ezekiel 21:21 NIV)
70 "They ____ not, neither do they spin" (Matthew 6:28)
71 "The men. . .which ____ him in the killing of his brethren" (Judges 9:24)
72 "Then Samuel took a ____ of oil" (1 Samuel 10:1)
73 Compass point (abbr.)
74 DANIEL'S FRIENDS WERE CAST INTO THIS TYPE OF FURNACE (Daniel 3:21)
75 "Some of them of understanding shall fall, to ____ them, and to purge" (Daniel 11:35)

DOWN

1 Makes mistakes
2 Fictional bear
3 ____ mater
4 Echolocation
5 Trailed

6. "Be not _____ with thy mouth" (Ecclesiastes 5:2)
7. Terminal abbreviation
8. "These are _____ without water" (2 Peter 2:17)
9. Wine bottle cap
10. Paul and Timothy weren't to preach the word here (Acts 16:6)
11. "As a bird that wandereth from her _____" (Proverbs 27:8)
13. "I have _____ thee in right paths" (Proverbs 4:11)
15. DANIEL WAS DELIVERED FROM THEM
20. "They shall _____ from the dead" (Mark 12:25)
22. Rowing aid
25. Heavy coat
26. GOD SENT THIS TO SHUT THE LIONS' MOUTHS (Daniel 6:22)
27. "I shall not _____, but live, and declare the works of the LORD" (Psalm 118:17)
29. Boredom
30. Formerly known as
32. "I will sacrifice unto thee with the _____ of thanksgiving" (Jonah 2:9)
33. Aggressively determined

34. "Give unto the LORD the glory _____ unto his name" (Psalm 96:8)
35. To dawdle
37. "The _____ head fell into the water" (2 Kings 6:5)
39. "That which groweth of _____ own accord of thy harvest" (Leviticus 25:5)
42. Compass point (abbr.)
43. BIBLICAL CHARACTER KNOWN FOR HIS ADVERSITIES
47. Lake
49. Row
50. Choose
52. More dignified
55. "They take away the _____ from the hungry" (Job 24:10)
57. Overgrown
58. Divisions of a tennis match
59. Country in SE Asia
60. _____ Canal
61. Assistant
62. Winter month (abbr.)
63. Discharge
64. Tackle
65. JOB'S SERVANT WAS THE _____ ONE TO ESCAPE THE CHALDEANS (Job 1:17)
68. Roman dozen

121

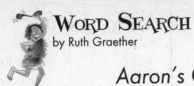

WORD SEARCH
by Ruth Graether

Aaron's Golden Calf
EXODUS 32

AARON
ALTAR
BRAKE
BREAK
BURNT OFFERINGS
CONSECRATE
CORRUPTED
DANCING
DRINK
EARRINGS
EGYPT
FEAST
FIRE
FORGIVE
GAVE
GODS
GOLD

GRAVING TOOL
HAND
ISRAEL
LAND
LORD
MOSES
PEACE
PEOPLE
PLAY
REPENTED
SACRIFICED
SEED
SELF
SIN
STARS
WAR
WRATH

```
D R M O D W E S D N C W S G S
Q A S O R N O G L S O W A R G
E D N A S F K N O T N R F B N
K K T C C E I I G A S L A C I
A H N M I R S R V R E N O A R
R D V I A N I E E S C R L F R
B T R T R E G F I G R V A O A
G S L O X D I F I U A O L R E
A A Z Y L V P O P C T M T G G
V E R E P E N T E D E S T I O
E F H Z O P E N S I N D E V D
E G Y P T D P R P E A C E E S
J P L A Y K U U K A E R B B D
M E D N A H Y B L E A R S I A
G R A V I N G T O O L D N A L
```

Sudoku
by Sara Stoker

Preparing Moses

DIFFICULT

	A	B	C	D	E	F	G	H	I
1	O					A		U	H
2	G		H	T			D		
3		U		O			G		
4	U				R		H		A
5			C	A		T			
6		T				G		C	
7			A				C		
8	C	O	G	R			A		U
9			U		A	C	O		

Hint: Column 2

"And he put forth his hand, and _____ it, and [the serpent] became a _____ in his hand" (Exodus 4:4).

The Birth of Jesus
SEE LUKE 2:16

Sometimes by following our star, we come across amazing things. Work this drop two puzzle to find out what some lowly shepherds discovered in a Bethlehem shed.

FRAILTY	Pathway	_____	1. ____ ____
OPALINE	Jail Punishment	_____	2. ____ ____
UNSTRAP	Portions	_____	3. ____ ____
GRINDER	Equestrian	_____	4. ____ ____
DIBASIC	Fundamental	_____	5. ____ ____
TWANGED	Fought	_____	6. ____ ____
HEATHER	Anesthetic	_____	7. ____ ____
EMERGED	Excessive desire	_____	8. ____ ____
ABALONE	Solitary	_____	9. ____ ____
ALCORAN	Reef	_____	10. ____ ____
BRACING	Mound of stones	_____	11. ____ ____
EASTERN	Mountain lakes	_____	12. ____ ____
LIGHTER	Octave	_____	13. ____ ____

____ ____ ____ ____ ____ ____ ____ ____ ____ ____ ____ ____ ____

1 2 3 4 5 6 7 8 9 10 11 12 13

ACROSTIC
by Donna K. Maltese

One, Two, Three, Testing

Sometimes we need confirmation of our godly commission. Solve this puzzle to discover how Gideon requested God's assurance via "sign language."

God called Gideon a "mighty man of _____." (Judges 6:12)

<u> </u> <u> </u> <u> </u> <u> </u> <u> </u> <u> </u>
19   39   32   27   14   8

Enemies of Israel (Judges 6:6)

20   9   33   41   38   30   15   7   1   26

Bearing sheep's fur

36   22   5   18   11

Tribe of Israel (Judges 6:35)

10   21   16   2   29   34   42   25

Removing doubt

31   40   35   28   17   6   37   23   4   12

Foreign god (Judges 6:25)

13   43   24   3

3-1-29   20-1   16-8-40-19-1,   41   16-8-39-11   7-2-1-1,

13-14-7   7-2-9-26   27-35-31-1   36-25-7-2   7-2-1

28-18-1-1-31-1;   3-1-29   15-7   10-5-36   13-1   33-6-11

27-30-32-11   14-16-22-4   7-2-1   28-18-1-1-31-1,

21-4-33   14-16-22-4   24-42-42   7-2-1   12-6-5-14-4-33

3-1-29   7-2-1-6-1   13-1   33-1-36.

JUDGES 6:39

CROSSWORD
by David K. Shortess

A Snake in the Grass

The theme answer is a long, familiar Bible quote that snakes up and down and back and forth and across the grid, even jumping across black squares. Follow the arrows and stay within the shaded squares.

Thou art cursed above all cattle, and above every beast of the field; upon thy belly shalt thou go.

GENESIS 3:14

ACROSS

1 START OF QUOTE FROM GENESIS 3 (see note above)
5 PART OF QUOTE
9 PART OF QUOTE
14 "And ____ bare Jabal" (Genesis 4:20)
15 "_____ abhor me" (Job 30:10)
16 Wealthy or powerful person
17 "Or clothe his neck with a flowing ____?" (Job 39:19 NIV)
18 Negative replies
19 Recover metal by heating ore
20 "The LORD shall judge the ____ of the earth" (1 Samuel 2:10)
21 Charlotte Brontë's Jane and family
23 Asian inland sea
24 PART OF QUOTE
25 Oklahoma town
27 Avenue crossers (abbr.)
30 "____ to your faith virtue" (2 Peter 1:5)
32 PART OF QUOTE
36 "Round about the ____ thereof" (Exodus 28:33)
37 "I know it ____ of a truth" (Job 9:2) (2 words)
39 "For whether is ____" (Matthew 9:5)
40 Ecology watchdog group (abbr.)
41 PART OF QUOTE
43 "They ____ the ship aground" (Acts 27:41)
44 "Now learn this ____ from the fig tree" (Matthew 24:32 NIV)
46 "Ye shall find a colt ____" (Mark 11:2)
47 "We ____ many" (Mark 5:9)
48 PART OF QUOTE
49 "Jerusalem, ____, she is broken" (Ezekiel 26:2)
50 Manuscripts (abbr.)

51 "As it had been the face ____ angel" (Acts 6:15) (2 words)
53 PART OF QUOTE
55 "____ do all things through Christ" (Philippians 4:13) (2 words)
58 "Who will ____ us?" (Isaiah 6:8) (2 words)
61 Expression of annoyance
65 Natives of northern Ohio, once
67 Friskies rival
68 "Why should ____ with thee?" (2 Samuel 13:26) (2 words)
69 "Get a new ____ on life" or start over
70 Afrikaans, language of South Africa
71 Swiss river
72 PART OF QUOTE
73 PART OF QUOTE
74 PART OF QUOTE

DOWN

1 "He shall have no ____ in the street" (Job 18:17)
2 "Thy god, ____, liveth" (Amos 8:14) (2 words)
3 Baton
4 PART OF QUOTE
5 PART OF QUOTE
6 Nautical greeting
7 "O thou ____, go, flee thee away" (Amos 7:12)
8 "That thou wilt not cut off ____ after me" (1 Samuel 24:21) (2 words)
9 ____ and offs
10 Southwestern covered porches
11 Salah's son (Genesis 10:24)
12 Alone (Sp.)
13 PART OF QUOTE
22 Tin in Chemistry 101

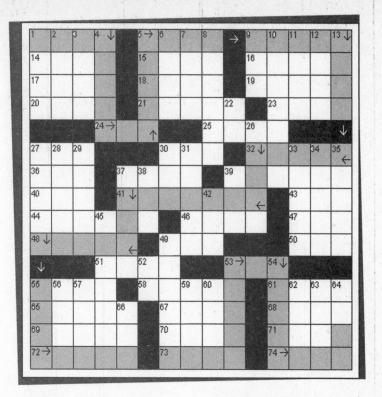

26 "Shall go ____ out" (John 10:9) (2 words)
27 Off-the-____ (not custom-made)
28 Conical abode
29 "____ her jugs" (Jeremiah 48:12 NIV)
30 Abijam's son (1 Kings 15:8)
31 "This man ____ many miracles" (John 11:47)
33 "Solomon sent to ____, saying" (1 Kings 5:2)
34 "They that sow in ____ shall reap in joy" (Psalm 126:5)
35 Sea eagles
37 "Let them break ____" (Exodus 32:24) (2 words)
38 Nine-digit ID (abbr.)
39 "Mine ____ is consumed because of grief" (Psalm 6:7)
42 U.S. Native American agency
45 "Over these ____ have buried here" (Jeremiah 43:10 NIV) (2 words)
49 "As he that feareth ____" (Ecclesiastes 9:2) (2 words)
52 Ashcroft, e.g. (abbr.)
53 PART OF QUOTE

54 PART OF QUOTE
55 PART OF QUOTE
56 "Immediately the cock ____" (Matthew 26:74)
57 Rizpah's mother, Saul's concubine (2 Samuel 3:7)
59 "The wall of the city shall fall down ____" (Joshua 6:5)
60 Colorful tropical fish
62 Quantity of paper
63 Taj Mahal site
64 Having pedal digits
66 "In just a ____" (very shortly)

SCRAMBLED CIRCLE
by Ken Save

Slave Labor

Although our situations may go from bad to worse, God is with us through them all.

1. RNMIOF

2. SIHFNI

3. TDYSEOR

4. LBTIU

5. TSLDEEAO

6. NONOATMBIIA

7. TIYMGH

8. IATAGSN

9. ESEAL

10. NVSOII

Who sold Joseph to Potiphar in Egypt?

1. _ _ _ _ _ ◯

2. _ ◯ _ _ _ _

3. ◯ _ _ _ _ _ _

4. _ _ ◯ _ _

5. _ _ _ _ _ ◯ _ _

6. _ _ _ _ _ ◯ _ _ _ _ _

7. _ ◯ _ _ _ _

8. _ _ _ _ _ _ ◯

9. _ _ _ _ ◯

10. _ _ ◯ _ _ _

Answer: The _ _ _ _ _ _ _ _ _ _ _

Stories of the Miraculous

Everyone loves a good miracle story. Can you solve these spotty headlines to find three New Testament men who experienced something beyond the realm of normal, everyday reality?

MAN B●INDED WHILE TR●VELING
TO PER●EC●TE CHRISTIANS

— — — —

●LIND B●GG●R ●AN ●H●ILLED
BY JE●●S' HE●L●NG

— — — — — — — — —

INNOCEN● MAN FR●ED FROM CHAINS
AND P●ISON BY ANSW●RED ●RAYER

— — — — —

WORD SEARCH
by John Hudson Tiner

Army of One
1 SAMUEL 17:37, 42

David said **moreover**, The LORD **that delivered** me out of the paw of the **lion**, and out of the paw of the **bear**, he **will** deliver me out of the **hand** of **this** Philistine. And **Saul said unto** David, Go, and the LORD be **with thee**. . . . And **when** the **Philistine looked about**, and saw **David**, he **disdained** him: for he was but a **youth**, and **ruddy**, and of a **fair countenance**.

```
P T Z O G U P E O O E F A X Q
O H R S U W T V W J A F L U Y
B E I F I N D L R M D L X P Q
S E D L Y H T I M Z E M M W N
X B L E I A T O A B F Y X O I
D F A I R S R N F S H L W D C
E C N A N E T N U O C R U A E
N H T U O Y V I W S S S G D M
I J H V K B E I N Z D H O C E
A Q E V P F T T L E B Q X K S
D R S L T H A T K E K M D T J
S D W A I W B O Y D D U R D I
I N Q I U Q O P Q G G A O N K
D A V I D L U C X Q E T L F Q
W H E N A I T M L B J R D M Z
```

133

ACROSTIC
by Donna K. Maltese

Making Waves

Sometimes we have trouble recognizing God. Crack the code to find out how Jesus' appearance made waves for a boatload of frightened followers.

Seagoing vessel

$\overline{7}$ $\overline{23}$ $\overline{4}$ $\overline{15}$

Tasteless liquid

$\overline{10}$ $\overline{16}$ $\overline{21}$ $\overline{33}$ $\overline{6}$

Unbelief

$\overline{34}$ $\overline{28}$ $\overline{22}$ $\overline{14}$ $\overline{8}$

Trouble

$\overline{29}$ $\overline{17}$ $\overline{20}$ $\overline{1}$ $\overline{32}$ $\overline{36}$ $\overline{26}$ $\overline{11}$

Cognizance

$\overline{12}$ $\overline{5}$ $\overline{9}$ $\overline{24}$ $\overline{31}$ $\overline{2}$ $\overline{19}$ $\overline{27}$ $\overline{35}$

In some situations, Peter showed little of this

$\overline{25}$ $\overline{13}$ $\overline{18}$ $\overline{30}$ $\overline{3}$

1-5-34   10-3-2-5   8-3-2   19-36-7-29-36-15-20-35-7

7-13-10   3-36-32   24-16-31-12-36-5-27   9-5   8-3-2

7-2-17,   8-3-2-11   24-2-6-2   26-6-28-22-14-20-35-19,

7-13-11-36-5-27,   4-21   4-7   17   7-15-4-6-4-30;   1-5-34

8-3-2-11   29-6-18-33-19   28-22-30   25-9-6   25-33-13-6.
MATTHEW 14:26

ANAGRAM
by Paul Kent

Moses' Story

From babyhood on, Moses lived a pretty amazing life. Here are three important things from Moses' story in the book of Exodus. . . . Can you unscramble the letters to solve these anagrams?

No main suit

_ _ _ _ _   _ _ _ _ _

Cold flange

_ _ _ _ _ _ _   _ _ _ _

Uh bring buns

_ _ _ _ _ _ _   _ _ _ _

TELEPHONE SCRAMBLE
by Connie Troyer

In the Land of Pharaoh

Egypt was ruled by a man with a heart of stone. Crack the telephone codes to dig up more information about this land, out of which the Jews once made a mass Exodus.

MNO 6	GHI 4	JKL 5	DEF 3

DEF 3	ABC 2	MNO 6	GHI 4	MNO 6	DEF 3

PRS 7	DEF 3	DEF 3	PRS 7	DEF 3	ABC 2

PRS 7	JKL 5	ABC 2	TUV 8	DEF 3	PRS 7	WXY 9

PRS 7	ABC 2	PRS 7	ABC 2	GHI 4

JKL 5	MNO 6	PRS 7	DEF 3	PRS 7	GHI 4

MNO 6	GHI 4	PRS 7	GHI 4	ABC 2	MNO 6

DEF 3	PRS 7	DEF 3	ABC 2	MNO 6	PRS 7

CROSSWORD
by Sarah Lagerquist Simmons

Stories with a Purpose

Jesus and other wise men told stories to guide and teach their listeners. As you work this crossword, may you return to these notable biblical tales and allow their hidden meaning to increase your understanding.

Let the wise listen and add to their learning, and let the discerning get guidance for understanding proverbs and parables, the sayings and riddles of the wise.
PROVERBS 1:5–6

ACROSS
1 "The waters called he ____" (Genesis 1:10)
5 Crooked
10 JESUS TOLD A PARABLE ABOUT A SOWER WHO WENT OUT TO ____ SEEDS
13 Spin
15 French river
16 The very first woman
17 "Wild animals will like it just fine, filling the vacant houses with ____ night sounds" (Isaiah 13:21 MSG)
18 "Who hath. . .____ out heaven with the span" (Isaiah 40:12)
19 "Deliver thyself as a ____ from the hand of the hunter" (Proverbs 6:5)
20 "____ them loose from the grip of Egypt" (Exodus 3:8 MSG)
21 JESUS SAID HE IS THE ____ SHEPHERD
23 NATHAN USED A STORY TO MAKE ____ SEE HIS SIN
25 Buzz
26 Easels
28 "They take counsel together. . .they ____ to take away my life" (Psalm 31:13 NKJV)
31 "Ye shall not make any cuttings in your flesh. . .nor ____ any marks upon you" (Leviticus 19:28)
32 "Let the living bird ____ into the open field" (Leviticus 14:7)
33 "I will ____ unto the LORD" (Exodus 15:1)
34 Freedom (abbr.)
37 Margarine
38 " 'My beloved is like a gazelle or a young ____' " (Song of Solomon 2:9 NASB)
40 Rage
41 "Their lungs breathe out poison ____" (Psalm 5:9 MSG)

42 "A banana ____ lands them flat on their faces" (Psalm 37:14 MSG)
43 Unit for measuring precious gems
45 "These Gadites were the ____ of the crop" (1 Chronicles 12:14 MSG)
46 Capital of Albania
47 Legume husks
50 THE PRODIGAL SON WAS TREATED TO THIS FOR DINNER
51 "Her husband may confirm it or. . . ____ it" (Numbers 30:13 NASB)
52 JESUS TOLD ABOUT A MAN WHO WAS FORGIVEN OF A DEBT OF 10,000 TALENTS BUT PUT A MAN IN ____ THAT OWED HIM 100 PENCE
53 "He doesn't endlessly ____ and scold" (Psalm 103:9 MSG)
56 Restricted (abbr.)
57 "One cake of ____ bread" (Exodus 29:23)
60 Crumble
62 "Do ye not therefore ____, because ye know not the scriptures. . . ?" (Mark 12:24)
63 "The ____ of them that sing do I hear" (Exodus 32:18)
64 Large couch
65 Color
66 A WEDDING ____ WITHOUT THE PROPER GARMENT WAS CAST OUT OF THE WEDDING IN THIS STORY
67 "The One. . .has founded His vaulted ____ over the earth" (Amos 9:6 NASB)

DOWN
1 "There is but a ____ between me and death" (1 Samuel 20:3)
2 Pitcher
3 Breezy
4 ____ Lanka

5 PAUL WROTE THAT CHRISTIANS NEED TO PUT ON THE WHOLE ____ OF GOD, IN ORDER TO STAND AGAINST THE DEVIL
6 "Their feet are swift to ____ blood" (Romans 3:15)
7 Gear
8 Unsaturated carbon compound (suffix)
9 GUESTS INVITED TO A ____ WOULD NOT COME, SO THEY INVITED ANYONE THEY COULD FIND IN THIS STORY
10 Control system (abbr.)
11 Egg-shaped
12 "The ____ were wrapped about my head" (Jonah 2:5)
14 Bean
22 " 'I have made you a tester of metals and my people the ____' " (Jeremiah 6:27 NIV)
24 "Men of might. . . were strong and ____ for war" (2 Kings 24:16)
25 Mexican coin
26 Neat
27 Japanese money
28 Toil
29 Pop
30 "The charge was two-thirds of a shekel for the plowshares. . .and to fix the ____" (1 Samuel 13:21 NASB)
31 "David delivered first this ____ to thank the Lord" (1 Chronicles 16:7)

34 Turkish money
35 Iraq's neighbor
36 Second letter of Greek alphabet
38 JESUS TOLD A STORY ABOUT ____ THAT WAS CAST INTO STONY PLACES
39 Drinks
42 "Keep therefore his statutes. . .that thou mayest ____ thy days upon the earth" (Deuteronomy 4:40)
43 DAVID HAD BATHSHEBA'S HUSBAND ____
44 Noise a dog makes
45 Computer (abbr.)
46 Siamese
47 Blanched
48 IN PROVERBS, IT TELLS US THAT WISDOM CRIES OUT AT THE ____ OF THE CITY (Proverbs 8:3)
49 Benedict Arnold's coconspirator
50 Trainee
52 Strap used in falconry
53 Recent (Portuguese)
54 The first man
55 Basic unit of heredity
58 Debt
59 "If a soul sin. . .and ____ unto his neighbor" (Leviticus 6:2)
61 "I will ____ you out of their bondage" (Exodus 6:6)

WORD SEARCH
by David Austin

Shipwrecked
ACTS 27:41–44

And falling into a place where two **seas** met, they ran the **ship aground**; and the **forepart stuck fast**, and **remained unmoveable**, but the **hinder** part was **broken** with the **violence** of the **waves**. And the **soldiers' counsel** was to **kill** the **prisoners**, lest any of them should **swim** out, and escape. But the **centurion**, **willing** to **save Paul**, kept them from their **purpose**; and **commanded** that they which could swim should **cast themselves** first into the sea, and get to **land**: And the **rest**, some on **boards**, and some on broken **pieces** of the ship. And so it came to pass, that they **escaped** all **safe** to land.

```
Z  H  E  S  O  P  R  U  P  W  A  P  I  D  P
Q  J  C  P  U  A  S  N  I  A  S  W  I  M  U
K  L  N  O  N  S  A  F  E  V  U  I  C  B  R
H  N  E  N  M  Z  V  Z  C  E  K  L  W  R  C
H  L  L  W  O  M  E  U  E  S  C  L  W  O  O
Y  L  O  W  V  L  A  B  S  C  U  I  U  K  C
L  Z  I  C  A  S  T  N  S  A  T  N  S  E  E
D  D  V  L  B  R  S  R  D  P  S  G  R  N  N
X  J  N  L  L  S  E  V  L  E  S  M  E  H  T
Q  F  A  U  E  N  R  M  L  D  D  D  I  G  U
E  U  A  F  O  R  E  P  A  R  T  N  D  N  R
S  E  A  S  D  R  A  O  B  I  R  A  L  H  I
H  A  I  K  T  Y  G  L  T  F  N  L  O  C  O
I  R  E  D  N  I  H  A  D  R  I  E  S  U  N
P  R  S  E  F  B  N  W  U  K  E  E  D  A  I
```

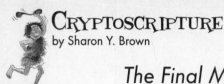

The Final Moments

Jesus came to earth to show us the way to God. Solve these cryptoscriptures to discover details of Jesus' final moments on the cross as He made the ultimate sacrifice.

KSR VJDKLB UHCLB K LJLDB, KSR VAL JL CS LGB

MHCQQ. KSR LGB UHJLJST UKQ, OBQAQ CW

SKIKHBLG LGB XJST CW LGB OBUQ.

VYC QAOY UOBZB AVC TPEOC QEJA V XGZC

FGETO, AO BVEC, HVJAOP, EYJG JAN AVYCB E

TGWWOYC WN BSEPEJ: VYC AVFEYR BVEC JAZB,

AO RVFO ZS JAO RAGBJ.

SUDOKU
by Sara Stoker

The Philistines and God's Judgment

MEDIUM

	A	B	C	D	E	F	G	H	I
1	H	O	N				K	A	E
2			E		O	N			H
3			T				R		N
4	O	R	G		T		A		
5	E	H					N		
6	T	N	K		A		G		
7					G		O		
8	N				H			T	A
9		E	R			T	H	K	G

Hint: Row 3

Two of the five Philistine capital cities under God's judgment were
_____ and _____ (1 Samuel 5:8–10).

ACROSTIC
by Donna K. Maltese

It's a Family Affair

Decipher this puzzle to find out which son of David's was literally lovesick.

Tamar's dad (1 Chronicles 3:9)

——— ——— ——— ———   ——— ——— ——— ——— ———
20   4   13   33   10   19   30   24   16

Jonadab to Amnon (2 Samuel 13:3)

——— ——— ——— ——— ——— ———
31   6   29   8   23   15

To grow in intensity

——— ——— ———
25   2   35

David to Amnon (2 Samuel 3:2)

——— ——— ——— ——— ——— ———
28   17   9   1   21   7

What Amnon resorted to

——— ——— ——— ——— ———
32   26   12   5   22

Sullen

——— ——— ——— ——— ——— ———
11   18   27   14   34   3

19-11-13-18-13   25-17-8   34-14   30-21-35-21-16,

9-1-2-9   1-21   28-21-32-32   34-24-31-20   28-6-27

1-24-34   8-4-8-9-3-7   9-17-11-17-7;   28-6-27   8-1-3

25-17-8   2   30-12-7-33-12-15;   2-5-10   19-11-13-18-13

9-1-6-29-22-1-9   23-9   1-2-7-16   28-6-27   1-24-11   9-14

10-14   2-5-26-9-1-23-5-22   9-14   1-3-7.

2 SAMUEL 13:2

CROSSWORD

by David K. Shortess

Bethlehem's Visitors

From near and far, people came to see the Christ child born in Bethlehem. Can you solve this puzzle to find the names or descriptions of those who made the manger pilgrimage?

And thou Bethlehem. . .out of thee shall come a Governor, that shall rule my people Israel.
MATTHEW 2:6

ACROSS

1 Brig occupant
5 "Who passing through the valley of ____ make it a well" (Psalm 84:6)
9 "If he arrives ____ will come with him to see you" (Hebrews 13:23 NIV) (2 words)
14 Puerto ____
15 Maj. Hoople's favorite expression
16 "But the ____ are the children of the wicked one" (Matthew 13:38)
17 U.S. island occupied by Japan during WWII
18 Goulash
19 Bathsheba's first husband (2 Samuel 11:3)
20 VISITORS (Luke 2:15) (2 words)
23 "Yet we did ____ him stricken" (Isaiah 53:4)
24 Mr. Charles
25 O.T. book (abbr.)
28 Scale notes
29 Deteriorate
32 "Praise thy ____ Zion" (Psalm 147:12) (2 words)
33 City from which David took "exceeding much brass" (2 Samuel 8:8)
34 Corolla component
35 MORE VISITORS (Luke 2:4–7) (3 words)
40 "You are worried and ____ about many things" (Luke 10:41 NIV)
41 "The Philistines gathered ____ Dammim" (2 Samuel 23:9 NIV) (2 words)
42 Mend, as a sock
43 Open, as a flag
45 Weasel
48 Golfer Ernie
49 Menlo Park monogram
50 Electrical unit
52 MORE VISITORS (Matthew 2:1–11) (3 words)
55 Stockpile
58 Mariner who discovered Cape of Good Hope
59 Bye-bye
60 "Whom shall ____" (Psalm 27:1) (2 words)
61 Sea eagle
62 Land west of Nod (Genesis 4:16)
63 In accord (2 words)
64 "But in ____ and in truth" (1 John 3:18)
65 "And Jacob ____ his clothes" (Genesis 37:34)

DOWN

1 Top drawer
2 "Compassed about ____ great a cloud of witnesses" (Hebrews 12:1) (2 words)
3 Musical groups
4 Despicable person
5 "Behold now ____, which I made with thee" (Job 40:15)
6 "I had rebuilt the wall and not ____ was left in it" (Nehemiah 6:1 NIV) (2 words)
7 Not "plastic"
8 Stick like glue
9 "____ to show thyself approved unto God" (2 Timothy 2:15)
10 "Wherein shall go no galley with ____" (Isaiah 33:21)
11 "Give light to my eyes, ____ will sleep in death" (Psalm 13:3 NIV) (2 words)
12 Education assn.
13 Like (suffix)

21 What Jesus did at Lazarus's tomb (2 words)
22 "They ____ the ship aground" (Acts 27:41)
25 "But he answered her ____ word" (Matthew 15:23) (2 words)
26 "The twelfth month, which is the month ____" (Esther 3:13)
27 "Sacrifice, ____, acceptable unto God" (Romans 12:1)
30 British rule in India
31 Quiverful
32 Rubies, for example
33 Has ____, kin of also ran
34 "In ____ and hymns and spiritual songs" (Colossians 3:16)
35 Revelation preceder
36 Iridescent gem
37 Belonging to Lithuania and Estonia, once (abbr.)
38 Former cabinet secretary Udall, to his friends
39 "His hand is still ____" (Isaiah 10:4 NIV)
43 Egypt and Syria, once (abbr.)
44 Required

45 Created again
46 "The ten horns which thou sawest ____ kings" (Revelation 17:12) (2 words)
47 Apartment dweller, often
49 "And God said, Let ____ be light" (Genesis 1:3)
51 Andrew's brother
52 Comparison word
53 Ireland, formerly
54 "And your moon will ____ no more" (Isaiah 60:20 NIV)
55 Mole's milieu? (abbr.)
56 Exchange student organization (abbr.)
57 Company bigwig (abbr.)

DROP TWO
by Dorothy Pryse

Paul's Journeys
SEE ACTS 27:15

Oftentimes Paul journeyed into troubled waters. Fortunately, he knew Jesus would keep him afloat. Solve this puzzle to find out how Paul's boat was faring off the shores of Crete.

TRADING   Empty   _____   1. ____ ____

HUSHING   Employing   _____   2. ____ ____

EMITTED   Speed recorded   _____   3. ____ ____

UNASKED   Nude   _____   4. ____ ____

HAPLESS   Price cuts   _____   5. ____ ____

IONIZED   Area coded   _____   6. ____ ____

PLANTER   Not now   _____   7. ____ ____

WROUGHT   Coarse   _____   8. ____ ____

ADENOID   Ate   _____   9. ____ ____

WHISKED   Walked   _____   10. ____ ____

INSCAPE   Windows   _____   11. ____ ____

NAMABLE   Stroll   _____   12. ____ ____

USHERED   Transparent   _____   13. ____ ____

__ __ __ __ __ __ __ __ __ __ __ __ __

1   2   3   4   5   6   7   8   9   10   11   12   13

BIBLE QUOTATION
by Suzanne Stepp

A Memorable Meal
LUKE 22:19–20

Work this Bible quotation puzzle to decode a memorable meal the disciples could not pass over.

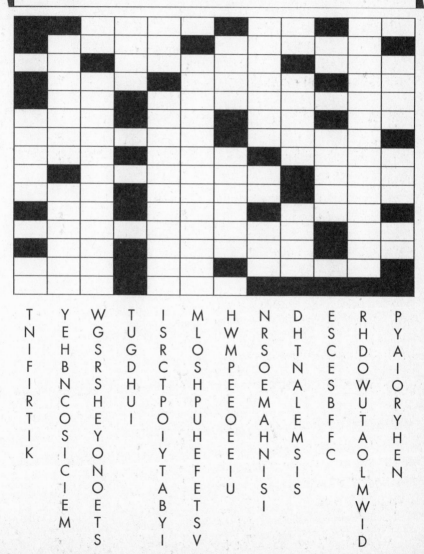

T	Y	W	T	I	M	H	N	D	E	R	P
N	E	G	U	S	L	W	R	H	S	H	Y
I	H	S	G	R	O	M	S	T	C	D	A
F	B	R	D	C	S	P	O	N	E	O	I
I	N	S	H	T	H	E	E	A	S	W	O
R	C	H	U	P	P	O	M	L	B	U	R
T	O	E	I	O	U	E	A	E	F	T	Y
I	S	Y		I	H	E	H	M	F	A	H
K	I	O		T	E	I	N	S	C	O	E
	C	N		A	F	U	I	I		L	N
	I	O		B	E		S	S		M	
	E	E		Y	T			I		W	
	M	T		I	S					I	
		S			V					D	

WORD SEARCH
by Connie Troyer

Bringing Up the Axe
2 KINGS 6:1–7

ALAS
AXE HEAD
BEAM
BORROWED
CAST
CONTENT
CRIED
CUT DOWN
ELISHA
FELLING
HAND
IRON
JORDAN
MAN OF GOD
MASTER

PLACE
PROPHETS
PUT
SERVANTS
SHEWED
SONS
STICK
SWIM
TAKE
THEE
THITHER
TOOK
WATER
WHERE
WOOD

```
T O K A E K A T H I T H E R A
D O R E C A L P R O U I L T U
E T A D U X O J E N O R I R T
W B N A L C U T D O W N S E N
E A E R N K A E T P L O H T E
H R S O A O W S A U N B A A T
S P W E D O K O T S D A L W N
F O I O R T H N O V A T I H O
E P M R O V R T A D E U R E C
L H O E J E A S T E H P O R P
L B W A T B E N O N E R K E D
I E J S R O B S T Y X I C E I
N X A P T H E E F S A M I L K
G M O R S S A L A U S R T E T
A L D O G F O N A M C A S O C
```

ACROSTIC
by Donna K. Maltese

Troubled Waters

Jesus is our bridge over troubled waters. Decipher this puzzle to uncover a certain man's plea for Jesus' help at Bethesda.

Day of rest

$\overline{19}$ $\overline{8}$ $\overline{14}$ $\overline{29}$ $\overline{34}$ $\overline{1}$ $\overline{25}$

Free of defect

$\overline{24}$ $\overline{6}$ $\overline{11}$ $\overline{35}$ $\overline{17}$

Feast of the Jews (John 2:13)

$\overline{10}$ $\overline{20}$ $\overline{13}$ $\overline{31}$ $\overline{2}$ $\overline{18}$ $\overline{7}$ $\overline{26}$

Crippled

$\overline{32}$ $\overline{21}$ $\overline{4}$ $\overline{15}$

Length of time something lasts

$\overline{16}$ $\overline{28}$ $\overline{9}$ $\overline{33}$ $\overline{30}$ $\overline{27}$ $\overline{22}$ $\overline{3}$

Recline

$\overline{23}$ $\overline{5}$ $\overline{12}$

1-25-17   27-4-10-11-30-12-3-30   4-21-3

33-3-19-24-7-9-7-16 6-5-4, 31-5-26, 27 6-34-18-15

3-22 4-21-3, 24-6-7-3 1-25-17 24-20-30-7-26 5-13

30-9-22-28-14-32-7-16, 1-22 10-28-30 4-7 5-3-1-22

1-25-17 10-2-2-23.

JOHN 5:7

CROSSWORD
By David K. Shortess

Some Parables of Jesus

Everyone loves a good story, and Jesus' listeners were no exception. Can you solve this parable-filled puzzle to uncover four story topics told by Jesus?

And with many such parables spake he the word unto them, as they were able to hear it.

MARK 4:33

ACROSS

1 "Beau ____"
6 Part of centerpiece
10 Belonging to good king of Judah
14 Top story?
15 Smidgen
16 Where Jesus met the Samaritan woman
17 "So that a bow of ____ is broken" (2 Samuel 22:35)
18 Care facility workers (abbr.)
19 ____ bellum
20 PARABLE (Luke 18:2–8) (2 words)
23 Architect I.M. ____
24 "For ____ stiffnecked people" (Exodus 34:9) (3 words)
25 PARABLE (Luke 10:30–37) (2 words)
32 Money, biblically
33 Radio host Limbaugh
34 Test for some seniors (abbr.)
37 Tolkien's bad guys
38 Queen of ____, Solomon's guest
40 "And fashioned it with a graving ____" (Exodus 32:4)
41 "Be prepared" organization (abbr.)
42 Chow ____
43 "How ____ that day will be" (Jeremiah 30:7 NIV)
44 PARABLE (Matthew 25:31–46) (3 words)
48 "____ sending you out like lambs" (Luke 10:3 NIV) (3 words)
50 Keats product
51 START OF PARABLE (Matthew 13:3–9) (4 words)
59 Left ____, in Paris
60 Despise
61 "How right they are to ____ you" (Song of Solomon 1:4 NIV)

62 S-shaped molding
63 Sea eagle
64 "That the aged men be ____" (Titus 2:2)
65 Comedian Foxx
66 "As ____ man who casteth firebrands" (Proverbs 26:18) (2 words)
67 Cornered

DOWN

1 "I cry out, I ____ and pant" (Isaiah 42:14 NIV)
2 Major ending
3 Follower of young or old alike
4 Bow and ascot
5 Solar, for one
6 "Then you will become their ____" (Habakkuk 2:7 NIV)
7 Top drawer
8 Funny man Laurel, familiarly
9 "On the ____ of Eden" (Genesis 4:16)
10 "And we eagerly ____ Savior" (Philippians 3:20 NIV) (2 words)
11 "Is the ____ message by the hand of a fool" (Proverbs 26:6 NIV) (3 words)
12 Choir members
13 "And they ____ bullock" (1 Samuel 1:25) (2 words)
21 Salt ____, biblical body
22 Away or back (comb. form)
25 Shapeless mass
26 Belonging to you and me
27 "I have ____ the death of all the persons of thy father's house" (1 Samuel 22:22)
28 Doctors (abbr.)
29 "Condemned to die in the ____" (1 Corinthians 4:9 NIV)
30 "There's the ____"

154

31 O.T. book
35 Lopsided win
36 Building additions
38 Understand
39 With it
40 "And she threw in ____ mites" (Mark 12:42)
42 Same, in Strasbourg
43 Get older rapidly (2 words)
45 Peddled
46 "I have ____ of you" (1 Corinthians 12:21 NKJV) (2 words)
47 Banned insecticide (abbr.)
48 Eva of "Green Acres"
49 Missouri river
52 Flightless bird
53 Cozy
54 Sicilian spewer
55 "By this time there is a bad ____" (John 11:39 NIV)
56 "And put on him a scarlet ____" (Matthew 27:28)
57 "Hast thou eaten of the ____" (Genesis 3:11)

58 "Into the ____ of swine" (Matthew 8:31)

SPOTTY HEADLINE
by Paul Kent and Sara Stoker

Husbands and Wives

You'll find more men than women on the pages of scripture, but the fairer sex is there, too—sometimes in the stories of married couples. Try to solve these spotty headlines relating to memorable wives and the men they married.

●U●T MAN T● WED ●IS
●REGNANT FIANC●E

— — — — — —

RU●ER'S W●F● S●EAKS UP FOR
MAN ●CCUSED OF ●REASON

— — — — — —

MAN'S WIFE BEC●MES SA●T S●ATUE

— — —

Lost and Found

If we seek Christ, we will find Him.

1. GSTUOH

2. FTAES

3. ZAEDMA

4. MAPCOYN

5. KFISNOKL

6. NSISBSEU

A young boy was found here.

1. _ _ _ _ _ ⃝
2. _ ⃝ _ _ _
3. _ ⃝ _ _ _ _
4. _ _ _ ⃝ _ _ _
5. _ _ _ _ _ _ ⃝ _
6. _ _ _ _ _ ⃝ _ _

Answer: _ _ _ _ _ _

Ark of Bulrushes
EXODUS 2:2–3; HEBREWS 11:23

The **woman conceived**, and **bare** a son: and when she saw him that he was a **goodly child**, she hid him **three months**. And when she **could** not **longer hide** him, she **took** for him an ark of **bulrushes**, and **daubed** it with **slime** and with **pitch**, and put the child **therein**; and she **laid** it in the **flags** by the **river's brink**. . . .

By **faith Moses**, **when** he was **born**, was hid three months of his **parents**, **because** they saw he was a **proper** child; and **they were** not **afraid** of the **king's commandment**.

```
R  G  M  Y  E  D  I  H  V  F  C  Y  G  S  B
E  T  C  R  S  H  T  N  C  O  W  F  Y  U  O
P  N  E  O  I  L  A  H  M  T  J  S  L  W  R
O  W  X  C  U  M  I  M  E  A  I  R  D  F  N
R  E  G  N  O  L  A  M  W  Y  U  P  O  L  H
P  O  E  W  D  N  D  S  E  S  O  M  O  A  W
N  U  P  R  D  A  C  B  H  T  S  C  G  G  Q
U  I  U  M  H  Q  D  E  B  U  A  D  H  S  A
U  A  E  Q  U  T  S  C  I  I  I  C  T  K  F
A  N  B  R  I  N  K  A  A  V  B  N  I  O  S
T  R  I  V  E  R  S  U  F  A  E  N  A  O  B
Z  M  O  N  T  H  S  S  R  R  G  D  F  T  U
P  X  E  Q  D  W  T  E  A  S  Y  U  L  I  W
Y  H  M  T  Q  L  W  P  I  Y  A  Y  V  X  M
W  L  W  J  V  L  A  I  D  V  G  R  G  J  P
```

ACROSTIC
by Donna K. Maltese

Waking the Dead

Jesus always takes care of those He loves. Solve this puzzle to find out who He helped get a "raise."

Town near Jerusalem (John 11:1)

$\overline{12}$ $\overline{35}$ $\overline{28}$ $\overline{3}$ $\overline{21}$ $\overline{8}$ $\overline{16}$

Astonish

$\overline{10}$ $\overline{19}$ $\overline{2}$ $\overline{25}$ $\overline{33}$

What Thomas's fellow disciples called him (John 11:16)

$\overline{9}$ $\overline{13}$ $\overline{22}$ $\overline{37}$ $\overline{32}$ $\overline{18}$ $\overline{7}$

Jesus performed this miracle so that God would be ____
(John 11:4)

$\overline{26}$ $\overline{17}$ $\overline{6}$ $\overline{23}$ $\overline{1}$ $\overline{29}$ $\overline{34}$ $\overline{20}$ $\overline{11}$

When Jesus witnessed His friends' grief, He did this (John 11:35)

$\overline{24}$ $\overline{4}$ $\overline{30}$ $\overline{15}$

Smell

$\overline{31}$ $\overline{5}$ $\overline{14}$ $\overline{36}$ $\overline{27}$

5-3-4-7-4   5-3-1-36-26-31   31-2-13-9   3-4:

2-8-11   2-29-15-35-23   5-3-2-5   3-4   31-2-13-5-3

18-36-28-6   5-3-4-19,   6-18-23   29-23-14-35-8-22

17-10-25-10-23-18-7   7-17-20-20-30-4-5-3;   12-18-28   1

26-6,   5-3-2-5   1   32-2-16   21-24-21-27-33   3-34-32

6-18-28   6-29   7-17-20-20-30.

JOHN 11:11

ANSWERS

Drop Twos

Born Again
BLEAT, SATIN, HATED, PLANT, ANGLE, GAILY, ARCED, PLATE, BOLES, BELLY, SHAVE, ADMIT

"Nicodemus, a ruler of the Jews." John 3:1

Sowing Seeds
WIDER, ACTED, BLAND, GRAIN, ARDOR, REMIT, CANAL, DRAWN, DRONE, VALET, EIGHT, CRATE

"When he sowed, some seeds fell." Matthew 13:4

Water Provided
CLEAN, MIDST, STAIN, CREAK, HOLEY, ROBES, NAMED, WANDS, BLAME, RAZED, TAINT, TRITE, TRICE

"Smite the rock, people may drink." See Exodus 17:6

Peter Jailed
GRANT, SCOUT, FIERY, ROVES, ODDER, DOWRY, SPADE, SHARP, STEIN, PRATE, FLOOR

"So Peter was kept in prison." See Acts 12:5

The Birth of Jesus
TRAIL, PENAL, PARTS, RIDER, BASIC, WAGED, ETHER, GREED, ALONE, CORAL, CAIRN, TARNS, EIGHT

"Found the babe lying in a manger." See Luke 2:16

Paul's Journeys
DRAIN, USING, TIMED, NAKED, SALES, ZONED, LATER, ROUGH, DINED, HIKED, PANES, AMBLE, SHEER

"The ship was caught up into wind." See Acts 27:15

ACROSTICS

Asp for Healing
FIERY, COMPLAINED, VENOMOUS, TYPE, PERISH, BETWEEN
"And Moses made a serpent of brass, and put it upon a pole, and it came to pass, that if a serpent had bitten any man, when he beheld the serpent of brass, he lived." Numbers 21:9

Spinning Wheels
VISION, BABYLON, PROPHET, FACES, WINGS, DUMB
"When the living creatures went, the wheels went by them: and when the living creatures were lifted up from the earth, the wheels were lifted up." Ezekiel 1:19

Miscommunication
TOGETHER, HUMANS, BUILD, TONGUE, SCATTER, FOIL
"Therefore is the name of it called Babel; because the LORD did there confound the language of all the earth." Genesis 11:9

Naaman's Lucky 7
CAPTAIN, LEPROSY, ELISHA, JEW, MAID, FORGIVENESS
"Then went he down, and dipped himself seven times in Jordan, according to the saying of the man of God." 2 Kings 5:14

A Gated Community
APOSTLES, VISION, GARNISHED, CHALCEDONY, FAITHFUL, TWELVE
"The twelve gates were twelve pearls: every several gate was of one pearl: and the street of the city was pure gold, as it were transparent glass." Revelation 21:21

A Story, a Story
VASHTI, CITIES OF REFUGE, NAZARITE, MEPHIBOSHETH, FIRSTBORN, WILDERNESS
"For whatsoever things were written aforetime were written for our learning, that we through patience and comfort of the scriptures might have hope." Romans 15:4

A Sign of Things to Come
KING, AMOZ, ASSYRIA, RECOVERED, HELP, WATERCOURSE
"In those days Hezekiah was sick to the death, and prayed unto the Lord: and he spake unto him, and he gave him a sign." 2 Chronicles 32:24

A Hot Topic
PARABLES, NETHERWORLD, CRUMB, TESTIFY, ZERO, GRIEVE
"Father Abraham, have mercy on me, and send Lazarus, that he may dip the tip of his finger in water, and cool my tongue." Luke 16:24

Redeeming Love
MAIZE, HANDFUL, GATHER, BARLEY, CLAN, LABORS
"Said Boaz unto Ruth, Hearest thou not, my daughter? Go not to glean in another field, neither go from hence, but abide here fast by my maidens." Ruth 2:8

A Bewitching Tale
PHILIP, WITCH, CRAFT, DEMONS, BEMUSE, SLY
"There was a certain man, called Simon, which beforetime in the same city used sorcery, and bewitched the people of Samaria." Acts 8:9

One Great Catch
TIBERIAS, FISHERMEN, DIRECTION, PETER, CAUGHT, WHOLLY
"Cast the net on the right side of the ship, and ye shall find. They cast therefore, and now they were not able to draw it for the multitude of fishes." John 21:6

Talk about Job Loss!
SERVANT, HEDGE, MISFORTUNE, BLEAK, WAY, CURSED
"Naked came I out of my mother's womb, and naked shall I return thither: the Lord gave, and the Lord hath taken away; blessed be the name of the Lord." Job 1:21

A Hair-Razing Tale
PHILISTINES, WEB, MANOAH, FIGURE, DAILY, CUT
"Delilah said to Samson, Tell me, I pray thee, wherein thy great strength lieth, and wherewith thou mightest be bound to afflict thee." Judges 16:6

One, Two, Three, Testing
VALOUR, MIDIANITES, WOOLY, NAPHTALI, CONFIRMING, BAAL
"Let me prove, I pray thee, but this once with the fleece; let it now be dry only upon the fleece, and upon all the ground let there be dew."
Judges 6:39

Making Waves
SHIP, WATER, DOUBT, CALAMITY, KNOWLEDGE, FAITH
"And when the disciples saw him walking on the sea, they were troubled, saying, It is a spirit; and they cried out for fear." Matthew 14:26

It's a Family Affair
KING DAVID, COUSIN, WAX, FATHER, LYING, MOROSE
"Amnon was so vexed, that he fell sick for his sister Tamar; for she was a virgin; and Amnon thought it hard for him to do anything to her."
2 Samuel 13:2

Troubled Waters
SABBATH, WHOLE, PASSOVER, LAME, DURATION, LIE
"The impotent man answered him, Sir, I have no man, when the water is troubled, to put me into the pool." John 5:7

Waking the Dead
BETHANY, AMAZE, DIDYMUS, GLORIFIED, WEPT, STINK
"These things said he: and after that he saith unto them, Our friend Lazarus sleepeth; but I go, that I may awake him out of sleep." John 11:11

WORD SEARCHES

Samson Defeats the Philistines

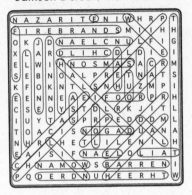

Ladder to Heaven

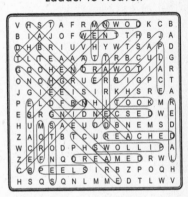

The Ark of the Covenant

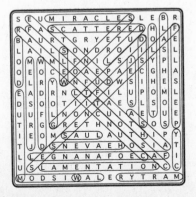

Stephen's Witness

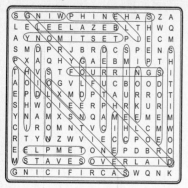

God Is Faithful in
the Old Testament

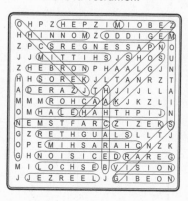

God Is Faithful in
the New Testament

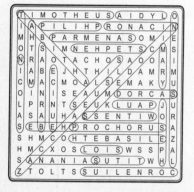

Joseph and Mary

Nathan's Parable

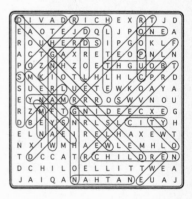

The Voyage Begins

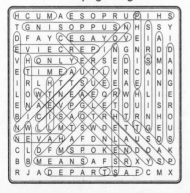

No Longer Doubting

Sodom and Gomorrah

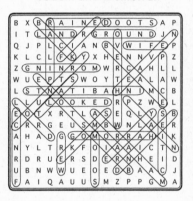

The Promised Land

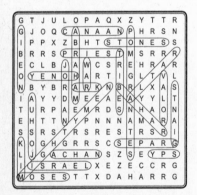

The Betrayer

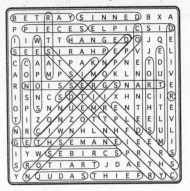

Aaron's Golden Calf

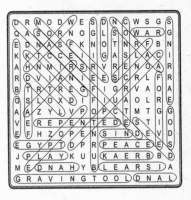

Army of One

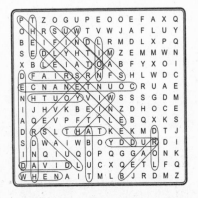

Shipwrecked

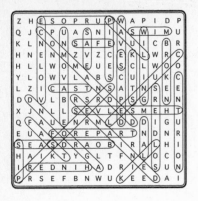

Bringing Up the Axe

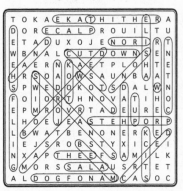

Ark of Bulrushes

CRYPTOSCRIPTURES

In the Days of Noah
"And God said unto Noah, The end of all flesh is come before me; for the earth is filled with violence through them; and, behold, I will destroy them with the earth." Genesis 6:13

"And of every living thing of all flesh, two of every sort shalt thou bring into the ark, to keep them alive with thee; they shall be male and female." Genesis 6:19

Before the Throne
"In the year that king Uzziah died I saw also the Lord sitting upon a throne, high and lifted up, and his train filled the temple." Isaiah 6:1

"Then said I, Woe is me! for I am undone; because I am a man of unclean lips, and I dwell in the midst of a people of unclean lips: for mine eyes have seen the King, the LORD of hosts." Isaiah 6:5

The Prophet and the Harlot
"And the LORD said to Hosea, Go, take unto thee a wife of whoredoms and children of whoredoms: for the land hath committed great whoredom, departing from the LORD." Hosea 1:2

"So he went and took Gomer the daughter of Diblaim; which conceived, and bare him a son. And the LORD said unto him, Call his name Jezreel." Hosea 1:3–4

To Show the Way

"And the LORD went before them by day in a pillar of a cloud, to lead them the way; and by night in a pillar of fire, to give them light; to go by day and night." Exodus 13:21

"And she shall bring forth a son, and thou shalt call his name JESUS: for he shall save his people from their sins." Matthew 1:21

Zechariah's Seventh Vision

"And I turned, and lifted up mine eyes, and looked, and, behold, there came four chariots out from between two mountains; and the mountains were mountains of brass." Zechariah 6:1

"And the angel answered and said unto me, These are the four spirits of the heavens, which go forth from standing before the Lord of all the earth." Zechariah 6:5

The Final Moments

"And Pilate wrote a title, and put it on the cross. And the writing was, JESUS OF NAZARETH THE KING OF THE JEWS." John 19:19

"And when Jesus had cried with a loud voice, he said, Father, into thy hands I commend my spirit: and having said thus, he gave up the ghost." Luke 23:46

SUDOKU

Ehud's Death

	A	B	C	D	E	F	G	H	I
1	S	E	D	A	T	C	L	O	F
2	C	T	O	L	S	F	D	E	A
3	L	A	F	O	E	D	S	C	T
4	A	S	T	F	L	O	E	D	C
5	O	F	E	C	D	T	A	S	L
6	D	C	L	S	A	E	T	F	O
7	E	D	C	T	F	L	O	A	S
8	F	L	A	D	O	S	C	T	E
9	T	O	S	E	C	A	F	L	D

FAT CLOSED

Jesus' Triumphal Entry

	A	B	C	D	E	F	G	H	I
1	O	E	T	D	S	N	A	K	Y
2	K	S	D	Y	A	O	N	T	E
3	Y	N	A	K	T	E	O	S	D
4	E	A	Y	T	D	S	K	O	N
5	S	T	N	E	O	K	Y	D	A
6	D	O	K	A	N	Y	S	E	T
7	A	D	S	N	K	T	E	Y	O
8	N	Y	O	S	E	D	T	A	K
9	T	K	E	O	Y	A	D	N	S

SAT/DONKEY

The Philistines and the Ark

	A	B	C	D	E	F	G	H	I
1	T	H	E	L	O	W	I	N	G
2	I	L	O	E	N	G	W	H	T
3	N	W	G	I	H	T	L	O	E
4	H	I	N	W	E	O	T	G	L
5	W	E	T	H	G	L	O	I	N
6	G	O	L	N	T	I	H	E	W
7	L	G	I	O	W	N	E	T	H
8	E	N	W	T	I	H	G	L	O
9	O	T	H	G	L	E	N	W	I

THE LOWING

Jezebel's Death

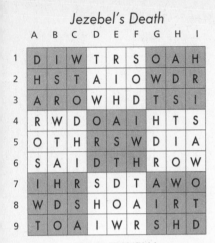

	A	B	C	D	E	F	G	H	I
1	D	I	W	T	R	S	O	A	H
2	H	S	T	A	I	O	W	D	R
3	A	R	O	W	H	D	T	S	I
4	R	W	D	O	A	I	H	T	S
5	O	T	H	R	S	W	D	I	A
6	S	A	I	D	T	H	R	O	W
7	I	H	R	S	D	T	A	W	O
8	W	D	S	H	O	A	I	R	T
9	T	O	A	I	W	R	S	H	D

SAID THROW

Preparing Moses

	A	B	C	D	E	F	G	H	I
1	O	C	R	D	G	A	T	U	H
2	G	A	H	T	C	U	D	O	R
3	D	U	T	O	H	R	G	A	C
4	U	G	D	C	R	O	H	T	A
5	R	H	C	A	D	T	U	G	O
6	A	T	O	H	U	G	R	C	D
7	T	R	A	U	H	O	C	D	G
8	C	O	G	R	T	D	A	H	U
9	H	D	U	G	A	C	O	R	T

CAUGHT ROD

The Philistines and God's Judgment

	A	B	C	D	E	F	G	H	I
1	H	O	N	T	R	G	K	A	E
2	R	K	E	A	O	N	T	G	H
3	G	A	T	H	E	K	R	O	N
4	O	R	G	N	T	H	A	E	K
5	E	H	A	G	K	O	N	R	T
6	T	N	K	R	A	E	G	H	O
7	K	T	H	E	G	A	O	N	R
8	N	G	O	K	H	R	E	T	A
9	A	E	R	O	N	T	H	K	G

GATH/EKRON

CROSSWORDS

Climbing the Walls

F	L	O	G		A	R	A	S	H		L	E	B	O

Across letters as shown:

FLOG ARASH LEBO
LINE SOMME ANEW
UPONTHETOWNWALL
TOE ONE MIE
SAWIN IST TREAT
AHOLEINTHEWALL
LAKE DOA GAY
ABE CARNIES OWL
AAH DDS ASEA
WALLOFBETHSHAN
CHILI LYS AHARD
OOS CIA ETA
WALLOFTHETEMPLE
AREA ALERT ELEV
TESS SYENE DOTE

Beauty Contest

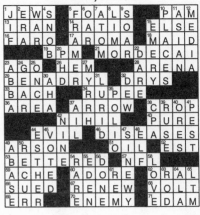

JEWS FOALS PAM
IRAN RATIO ELSE
FARO AROMA MAID
BPM MORDECAI
AGO HEM ARENA
BENADRYL DRYS
BACH RUPEE
AREA ARROW CROP
NIHIL PURE
EVIL DISEASES
ARSON OIL EST
BETTERED NFL
ACHE ADORE ORAL
SUED RENEW VOLT
ERR ENEMY EDAM

Nations in the Promised Land

JUST NAHUM SATA
ARAB IRATE OMER
CANAANITES LOST
ONE DES HEARTS
BILLS EGG MCI
SAYS GNAR BETTA
TOR LIMO EON
HUH HIVITES SOD
ISI IDOL ASH
METTO LENT ARFS
TWA TEA AMERE
ALIENS TED SIN
DATE PERIZZITES
ACED ADOOR GENE
MESS TOWNA ODDS

179

Characters of Parables and Stories

C	L	A	S	P		W	A	R	E		C	R	A	G
R	I	G	O	R		A	T	O	M		H	E	R	R
A	M	I	N	O		G	O	B	I		R	A	C	E
M	A	N		D	E	E	P		T	R	O	P	H	Y
		P	I	G	S		T	O	M					
V	I	R	A	G	O		S	T	E	W	A	R	D	
A	C	U	R	A		P	O	O	R		H	A	G	
L	I	B	E	L		T	U	G		A	M	I	G	O
E	N	E		R	A	T	S		T	E	N	O	N	
	G	N	O	M	I	S	H		S	T	R	O	N	G
	W	A	C			T	R	U	E					
S	T	A	N	C	H		C	H	I	N		M	C	G
H	O	W	E		M	A	L	I		I	D	A	H	O
A	G	A	R		A	K	I	N		N	A	M	E	D
W	A	Y	S		N	A	P	E		G	N	A	W	S

Windows of Opportunity

R	C	A		R	E	V		O	K	A		M	A	D
A	A	R		A	V	I	O	N	I	C		O	F	A
T	I	E		J	E	Z	R	E	E	L		N	O	V
O	R	N	O		O	S	A	V	E		T	R	I	
N	O	A	H	S	A	R	K		A	A	H	E	D	
			M	E	L		M	T	N	S				
A	S	A		E	L	A	T	E	R		T	I	L	E
T	O	W	A	R	D	J	E	R	U	S	A	L	E	M
E	X	E	C		I	A	T	E	I	T		L	I	T
			N	E	E	R		S	O	N				
T	O	W	E	L		D	A	M	A	S	C	U	S	
R	U	E		I	Z	A	R	S		F	A	T	E	
O	T	S		J	E	R	I	C	H	O		L	I	E
A	T	A		A	R	E	P	O	O	R		E	L	A
S	O	W		H	I	D		T	E	A		B	E	N

Animal Stories

M	A	R	C		A	L	U	L	A		S	U	B
A	G	U	A		P	I	P	E	R		B	O	L	O
N	O	E	L		O	Z	O	N	E		I	N	T	O
		F	M	G		N	O	A	H	S	A	R	K
B	O	N		P	E	A		I	O	T	A	S	
A	P	O	T	H	E	G	M		E	T	N	A	
B	E	A	U		G	O	A	T	S				
A	C	H	E		G	R	A	T	A		S	W	A	Y
		L	I	O	N	S		O	H	I	O		
	R	A	I	N		S	E	C	E	D	I	N	G
A	L	A	M	O		A	U	G		P	T	A	
D	E	M	A	N	D	E	D		T	O	N		
O	A	R	S		O	D	O	R	S		E	R	M	A
B	R	O	S		G	I	V	E		B	O	A	R
E	N	D		S	T	E	P	S		E	C	K	

Three Monetary Lessons

A	R	O	M	A		G	P	A		A	B	B	A
L	U	Z	O	N		R	A	W		C	L	O	D
A	L	O	S	T	C	O	I	N	F	O	U	N	D
K	E	N	T		R	A	N		A	R	E	N	A
E	R	E		B	E	N		O	W	N			
		T	E	E		B	A	N		T	A	J	
B	A	T	H	E		G	E	T		A	R	L	O
A	C	O	I	N	I	N	T	H	E	F	I	S	H
D	E	N	S		H	A	S		D	A	G	O	N
E	S	E		H	O	T		F	O	R			
		T	O	P		R	A	M		S	P	A	
S	T	R	I	P		S	O	N		M	A	I	N
T	H	E	W	I	D	O	W	S	M	I	T	E	S
A	R	E	A		O	W	E		A	M	O	C	O
B	U	D	S		E	N	D		L	I	N	E	N

Good Guys and Villains

C	A	R	L		C	R	O	P		H	A	R	P
A	L	O	E		S	W	A	M	I		A	G	U	E
L	A	M	A		N	A	S	A	L			T	D
F	R	E	S	C	O		P	H	A	R	A	O	H
			H	O	W	L		A	T	O	M		
F	A	O		H	E	A	D		E	D	I	C	T
L	T	D		E	D	G	A	R		R	O	B	E
A	L	I	G	N		E	V	E		H	E	R	O	D
P	A	U	L		R	I	F	L	E		N	N	E
	S	M	I	R	K		D	E	A	N		Y	E	N
		M	I	N	D		R	I	N	D			
	S	A	P	P	O	R	O		C	A	E	S	A	R
G	A	L	S		C	O	P	R	A		M	A	C	E
E	A	S	E		K	N	E	E	L		O	G	L	E
T	R	O	D		S	E	N	D		S	A	U	L

Alpha-Numeric Mix-Up

A	S	A		S	P	I	N		S	N	A	C	K	S
N	A	N		A	U	R	A		C	A	B	A	N	A
D	I	N		S	P	U	R		E	D	I	S	O	N
3	D	A	Y	S	A	N	D	3	N	I	G	H	T	S
		E	Y	E			O	E	R				
D	A	M	P		S	I	R		I	T	I	S	
I	S	A		T	H	O	R		S	O	R	R	O	W
A	N	D	T	H	E	S	E	3	A	R	E	O	N	E
N	E	A	R	E	R		N	O	T	E		V	I	E
A	R	M	Y		T	E	N		H	E	A	T		
		U	S	A			H	O	E				
3	M	E	A	S	U	R	E	S	O	F	M	E	A	L
M	I	L	L	E	R		L	A	S	T		A	B	A
E	R	M	I	N	E		A	L	E	E		S	L	Y
N	E	S	T	O	R		M	E	A	N		Y	E	S

On Trial

S	N	O	B	S		J	O	S	E		B	A	L	D
C	A	R	A	T		E	B	O	N		E	P	E	E
A	P	E	R	Y		S	I	D	E		R	A	V	E
M	E	S	A		C	U	E		M	A	R	R	E	D
		B	I	A	S		P	I	L	A	T	E		
W	O	B	B	L	Y		S	E	E	P				
A	U	R	A	L		H	A	R	S	H		E	H	F
C	R	O	S	S		A	G	O		A		L	I	E
S	S	W		G	N	A	T		B	A	S	T	E	
			D	U	D	S		D	E	T	E	S	T	
A	B	S		I	S		C	I	T	E				
U	P	L	I	F	T		D	A	M		L	O	S	S
S	H	A	M		A	C	A	D		A	I	S	L	E
D	I	D	O		R	U	L	E		B	E	L	O	W
A	D	E	N		S	P	I	T		C	R	O	W	N

Biblical Big Boys

G	U	A	M		S	A	L	E	M		B	A	R	E
A	G	R	A		O	C	A	L	A		E	N	O	S
T	H	E	R	E	W	E	R	E	G	I	A	N	T	S
		A	B	E	T		M	O	R	T				
N	E	T		B	R	I	M		G	A	L	O	R	E
A	L	O	G		C	E	O		E	R	E	I		
M	E	R	E	S	T		S	H	E	A		A	S	O
	G	O	L	I	A	T	H	O	F	G	A	T	H	
W	A	N		P	R	O	A		T	E	N	O	R	S
A	N	T	S		P	C	F		D	R	E	I		
S	T	O	W	E	D		H	U	L	A		Y	D	S
		A	R	E	A		L	E	S	S				
T	H	E	L	A	N	D	O	F	G	I	A	N	T	S
H	A	V	E		T	E	N	I	A		N	O	W	A
E	Y	E	S		S	N	E	L	L		D	R	O	P

A Double Portion

C	R	E	A	M		F	M	G		E	S	A	U
H	A	L	S	A		A	I	L		I	S	L	E	S
I	C	I	E	R		U	N	O		S	T	A	R	E
D	E	J	A		E	L	I	S	H	A		M	O	D
E	R	A		C	S	T		S	E	A	M			
	S	H	A	R	P		A	L	C	A	I	D	E	
		B	A	N		A	R	M		N	O	E	L	
J	A	C	O	B		S	T	Y		S	T	U	C	K
A	G	A	R		O	L	E		A	L	L			
P	O	T	T	A	G	E		P	O	E	T	S		
		S	I	R	E		S	S	W		A	P	T	
C	A	W		D	E	P	U	T	E		B	R	I	E
O	C	H	R	E		E	S	E		T	E	T	R	A
B	R	E	A	D		R	E	V		S	T	A	I	R
B	E	N	D			S	S	E		P	A	R	T	Y

182

Sowing the Word

Overcomers

A Snake in the Grass

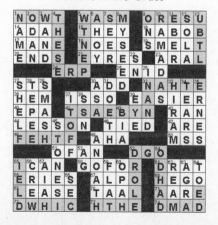

Stories with a Purpose

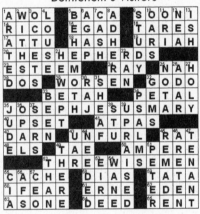

S	E	A	S			A	S	K	E	W		S	O	W
T	W	I	R	L		R	H	I	N	E		E	V	E
E	E	R	I	E		M	E	T	E	D		R	O	E
P	R	Y		G	O	O	D		D	A	V	I	D	
		P	U	R	R		T	R	I	P	O	D	S	
S	C	H	E	M	E		P	R	I	N	T			
L	O	O	S	E		S	I	N	G		L	I	B	
O	L	E	O		S	T	A	G		I	R	E		
G	A	S		P	E	E	L		K	A	R	A	T	
		C	R	E	A	M		T	I	R	A	N	A	
P	E	A	P	O	D	S		C	A	L	F			
A	N	N	U	L		J	A	I	L		N	A	G	
L	T	D		O	I	L	E	D		E	R	O	D	E
E	R	R		N	O	I	S	E		D	I	V	A	N
D	Y	E		G	U	E	S	T		D	O	M	E	

Bethlehem's Visitors

A	W	O	L		B	A	C	A		S	O	O	N	I
R	I	C	O		E	G	A	D		T	A	R	E	S
A	T	T	U		H	A	S	H		U	R	I	A	H
T	H	E	S	H	E	P	H	E	R	D	S			
E	S	T	E	E	M		R	A	Y		N	A	H	
D	O	S		W	O	R	S	E	N		G	O	D	O
			B	E	T	A	H		P	E	T	A	L	
J	O	S	E	P	H	J	E	S	U	S	M	A	R	Y
U	P	S	E	T		A	T	P	A	S				
D	A	R	N		U	N	F	U	R	L		R	A	T
E	L	S		T	A	E		A	M	P	E	R	E	
		T	H	R	E	E	W	I	S	E	M	E	N	
C	A	C	H	E		D	I	A	S		T	A	T	A
I	F	E	A	R		E	R	N	E		E	D	E	N
A	S	O	N	E		D	E	E	D		R	E	N	T

Some Parables of Jesus

G	E	S	T	E		V	A	S	E		A	S	A	S
A	T	T	I	C		I	O	T	A		W	E	L	L
S	T	E	E	L		C	N	A	S		A	N	T	E
P	E	R	S	I	S	T	E	N	T	W	I	D	O	W
			P	E	I			I	T	I	S	A		
G	O	O	D	S	A	M	A	R	I	T	A	N		
L	U	C	R	E		R	U	S	H		G	R	E	
O	R	C	S		S	H	E	B	A		T	O	O	L
B	S	A		M	E	I	N		A	W	F	U	L	
	S	H	E	E	P	A	N	D	G	O	A	T	S	
G	O	I	A	M			O	D	E					
A	S	O	W	E	R	W	E	N	T	F	O	R	T	H
B	A	N	K		H	A	T	E		A	D	O	R	E
O	G	E	E		E	R	N	E		S	O	B	E	R
R	E	D	D		A	M	A	D		T	R	E	E	D

Scrambled Circles

Ah, Hindsight
GOLIATH
He should have ducked. Who was he?
1. GREAT 2. HORSES 3. JEALOUS 4. MIDST 5. JERUSALEM
6. PLUMMET 7. HOSTS

A Story for the Grandkids
MEMORIAL
A pile of stones would serve as a way to remember a special event.
1. CONSUMED 2. MOCKED 3. MOUNT 4. ALLEGORY 5. TUTORS
6. MANIFEST 7. WEARY 8. FLESH

Would You Want This Job?
WASHED THEIR FEET
Jesus acted as His disciples' servant.
1. TOWEL 2. GARMENTS 3. HAND 4. HEAD 5. ASIDE 6. WATER
7. HOUR 8. WIPE 9. GIRDED 10. FEAST 11. SUPPER 12. PART

A Big Fish Tale
JONAH and the WHALE
Jesus made reference to this slimy story.
1. JESUS 2. SWORD 3. NETHER 4. LAMENT 5. PHARAOH 6. DWELT
7. TWELFTH 8. SLAIN 9. FALLEN 10. MULTITUDE

Slave Labor
THE MIDIANITES
Who sold Joseph to Potiphar in Egypt?
1. INFORM 2. FINISH 3. DESTROY 4. BUILT 5. DESOLATE
6. ABOMINATION 7. MIGHTY 8. AGAINST 9. LEASE 10. VISION

Lost and Found
TEMPLE
The young boy was found here.
1. SOUGHT 2. FEAST 3. AMAZED 4. COMPANY 5. KINSFOLK
6. BUSINESS

Anagrams

Important Locales
NINEVEH, MOUNT ARARAT, DAMASCUS

More Important Locales
GARDEN OF EDEN, JERICHO, MOUNT OF OLIVES

Scenes from the Exodus
PLAGUE OF BLOOD, DEATH OF FIRSTBORN, PARTING OF RED SEA

Jesus Was Here
LAST SUPPER, TRANSFIGURATION, ASCENSION

Moses' Story
MOUNT SINAI, GOLDEN CALF, BURNING BUSH

Spotty Headlines

Battle Stories
JOSHUA, ABSALOM, PHARAOH

Government Intrigue
HEROD, PILATE, DANIEL

They Met Jesus
SIMEON, ZACCHAEUS, NICODEMUS

Ruined Lives
ACHAN, ANANIAS, JUDAS

Stories of the Miraculous
SAUL, BARTIMAEUS, PETER

Husbands and Wives
JOSEPH, PILATE, LOT

Telephone Scrambles

Conversions
PAUL, RUTH, SAMUEL, CENTURION, PUBLICAN, ABRAHAM, CANAANITE

Thanks for Your Help
TYRANNUS, SAMARITAN, CYRUS, JONATHAN, OBADIAH, SHOBI, ABINADAB

Sound the Trumpets
PRAISE, JERICHO, WARNING, ZION, ANGELS, JUBILEE, EPHRAIM, GATHER

Cursed
CAIN, CANAAN, GROUND, NATURE, SERPENT, JUDAH

Allegories
HAGAR, LIONESS, SARAH, VINE, VINEYARD, GOMER

In the Land of Pharaoh
NILE, FAMINE, RED SEA, SLAVERY, SARAI, JOSEPH, MIRIAM, DREAMS

BIBLE QUOTATIONS

Tested by Fire
"He answered and said, Lo, I see four men loose, walking in the midst of the fire, and they have no hurt; and the form of the fourth is like the Son of God." Daniel 3:25

An Even Exchange
"Behold behind him a ram caught in a thicket by his horns: and Abraham went and took the ram, and offered him up for a burnt offering in the stead of his son." Genesis 22:13

Don't Look Back!
"But his wife looked back from behind him, and she became a pillar of salt." Genesis 19:26

The Best Birthday Ever
"For unto you is born this day in the city of David a Saviour, which is Christ the Lord." Luke 2:11

Answered Prayer
"Wherefore it came to pass, when the time was come about after Hannah had conceived, that she bare a son, and called his name Samuel, saying, Because I have asked him of the LORD." 1 Samuel 1:20

A Memorable Meal
"This is my body which is given for you: this do in remembrance of me. Likewise also the cup after supper, saying, This cup is the new testament in my blood, which is shed for you." Luke 22:19–20

Look for the entire
WORLD'S GREATEST BIBLE PUZZLES
collection!

Men of the Bible
978-1-60260-026-3

Women of the Bible
978-1-60260-027-0

Stories of the Bible
978-1-60260-029-4

Miracles of the Bible
978-1-60260-028-7

192 pages each / 5 ³⁄₁₆" x 8" / Paperback
Only $4.97 each!
Available wherever Christian books are sold.